The truth: Anti-Semitism and BDS two sides of the same coin

Second Edition, Volume 2

Daniel Farcas

Published by Daniel Farcas, 2024.

Introduction...5

"Jewish people were saved because The English Empire granted them a heaven for jews in Palestine"...............7

"Jewish terrorism" against English and Arabs"...9

"Armed Jews organized informal military armies to attacks and terrorize their Arabs neighbors".................12

"The jews expelled the Arabs from Palestine in Yom Haatzmaut/Nakba "...........................14

"Israel is perpetuating an Occupation"...16

"Israel is an Apartheid State"..17

"Israel is a state who abuses Women rights"...19

"Israel is a Racist state"...20

"Zionism is racism "..22

"Bedouins, Muslims, Christians and Druze don't enjoy full citizenship in Israel"................23

"Israel is a Colonialist state"..25

"Israel is an Imperialist state"...26

"Israel violates human rights"...28

"Israel committed genocide "..29

UNRWA and the real role of the UN...33

"LGTB+ are persecuted in Israel'..34

From the river to the sea, will be free...37

"Progressive left is acting responsibly in support of the Palestinians cause "...................40

Israel racism against blacks and other minorities...44

"Arabs leaders don't enjoy free of speech"...46

"In Israel there is not equal rights to different faiths"...................48

"Israel committed War crimes"...50

"Israel doing Ethnic cleansing "..51

"Israel committed war crimes"...53

"If Israel move to the 1967 borders will be peace"...59

"Israel its not equal rights state"arabs don't have the right to elect or to be elected"................61

"Jews have been persecuting and murdering arabs from the begging of the zionist movement "................62

"Arabs and muslims have been living in peace with jews worldwide."................64

"Jews live in peace today with Muslim n to address and prevent anti-Semitic attacks, ensuring the safety and security of Jewish communities.......67

"Anti israeli movements and demonstrations are not antisemitic "...............................67

"United Nations is a fair and trustable organization That treat Israel Like any other country "......................71

"Jews stole land from arabs"...............................71

"Jews bringed the malaria to Palestine"...............................74

"Jews stole the Palestinians Organs"...............................76

The UN fairly condemns Israel %...............................77

"Arabs were first in Palestine and Jesus was Palestinian "...............................79

"Arabs are the legitimate exclusive Heritage of Abraham Itzjak and Jacob "...............................83

"Jewish terrorism" against english and Arabs...............................91

" The armed jews organized military informal Armies in order to attacks their Arabs neighborhood and to terrorized them "94

Yom haatzmaut /Nakba , "the jews expelled the Arabs from Palestine"...............................97

Israel is perpetuating the Occupation...............................98

"Israel is an Apartheid State"...............................100

Israel machinist Patriarchal state "...............................102

"Israel is a state with many Women rights abuses "...............................102

"Israel is a Racist state"...............................103

"Zionism is racism "...............................105

"Israel committed genocide "...............................113

UNRWA and the real role of the UN...............................116

LGTB+ are persecuted in Israel...............................118

From the river to the sea, Palestine will be free...............................121

The Palestinian are the real victims...............................123

The left wing is equilibrate and don't have any bias against Israel...............................126

Israel racism against blacks and other minorities...............................128

"Arabs leaders don't enjoy free of speech"...............................131

"Israel committed War crimes"...............................134

"Israel doing Ethnic cleansing "...............................136

"BDS it's not an anti semitic instrument "...............................142

"Jews have been persecuting and murdering arabs from the begging of the zionist movement "..................147

"United Nations is a fair and trustable organization That treat Israel Like any other country "..................156

"Jews stole land from arabs"..................156

"Arabs worked the land and transform it in a productive one"..................157

"Jews bring the malaria to Palestine"..................159

"Jews stole the Palestinians Organs"..................161

The UN condemns Israel..................162

"Arabs were first in Palestine and Jesus was Palestinian "..................164

"Arabs are the legitimate exclusive Heritage of Abraham Itjak and Jacob "..................168

Gaza the biggest lail in the world..................170

Israel prevent Gaza to be the Songapure of the Middle East..................171

There is no proportionality regarding the israeli atack to Gaza..................172

.If Israel move to the 1967 borders will be peace"..................173

Acknowledgements

Sincere gratitud

Bar Ilan University:

• **Professor Michael Ehrlich: I am deeply grateful for your unwavering support and guidance throughout the entire writing process. Their experience and knowledge have greatly enriched this book.**

The Jewish Agency:

• **Revitale Einstein, Natalia Sidon and Ella Mirzaib: I extend my sincere gratitude to each of you for your valuable contributions and assistance. Their diverse perspectives and understandings have been indispensable in providing a comprehensive vision.**

Directors of the Jewish Community of Chile:

● Ariela Agosin, Daphne Englander, Gabriel Silber and Grace Agosin: I express my gratitude for your role in providing knowledge and perspectives of the Jewish community of Chile. Their support and collaboration have been essential to capturing the essence of their experiences.

Community of Chileans in Israel:

● Gabriel Colodro, Hernán López, Daniel Weinstein and Sivan Gobrin: I want to extend my deep gratitude to each of you from the community of Chileans in Israel. Their unwavering support and encouragement have been invaluable in shedding light on the experiences of Chileans living in Israel.

● My wife, Pamela Werbin:

I would like to acknowledge the incredible support and assistance provided by my wife, Pamela Werbin, throughout the entire process. Their unwavering dedication and faith in this project have been a constant source of motivation and inspiration.

● My mother, Clara Guendelman:

I would like to express my gratitude to my mother, Clara Guendelman, for her help with the translation and her continued support. Their unwavering faith in this project has been a guiding force

● To my Alberto Farcas, the intelligence and wisdom of my father but even more important ,its constant guide and unconditional support

● The Farcas Guendelman family

I extend my sincere thanks and gratitude to my parents, Alberto and Clara, and my siblings, David, Alan and Claudia. His unwavering commitment to Israel and his support of this project have been a constant source of inspiration.

Individuals and organizations promoting Israel:

● Ron Brumner: Thank you for your leadership in the fight against the new anti-Semitism and the BDS movement.

● Miriam Feinberg: I express my sincere gratitude to you for your steadfast defense of Israel's right to exist and live in peace.

● I want to also remark the significant job of Olga Nurie and her always willingness to help and collaborate with Hasbara

● MK Shareen Haskel: I am grateful for your tireless work and for your commitment to explain the truth about israel.

● Marion Reinengger the co-author of this book, has always worked hard and professionally. She is great!

Introduction

1 Israel, a small country in the Middle East, has been the subject of numerous lies, false information, and fake news over the years. These misconceptions and falsehoods have often been used to demonize and delegitimize the state of Israel, its people, and its policies. In this essay, we will explore some of the most common lies, false information, and fakes about Israel and examine their impact on public perception and discourse.

One of the most pervasive lies about Israel is the claim that it is an apartheid state. This accusation is based on the false premise that Israel systematically discriminates against its Arab citizens and denies them fundamental– rights and freedoms. Israel is a vibrant democracy with a diverse population that includes Arab citizens who enjoy equal rights under the law. Arab citizens of Israel serve in the Knesset of the Israeli parliament and hold positions of power and influence in various sectors of society. The accusation of apartheid is not only false but also deeply offensive to those who have experienced true apartheid in countries like South Africa.

Another common falsehood about Israel is the claim that it is an aggressive and expansionist state that seeks to conquer and occupy Arab lands. This narrative ignores the historical context of the Israeli-Conflict*and the numerous peace offers that Israel has made over the years to reach a peaceful resolution. Israel has repeatedly demonstrated its willingness to negotiate and compromise for the sake of peace, including withdrawing from territories like Sinai and Gaza in exchange for peace agreements. The accusation of expansionism is a distortion of the conflict rather than resolving it.

Fake news and misinformation about Israel are also prevalent in the media and on social media platforms. False claims about Israeli military actions, human rights abuses, and war crimes are often circulated without verification or context, leading to a skewed and biased portrayal of the Israeli-Palestinian conflict. It is essential for readers and viewers to critically evaluate the sources of information they consume and to seek out multiple perspectives in order to form a more accurate and nuanced understanding of complex issues like the Israeli-Palestinian conflict.

In conclusion, lies, false information, and fakes about Israel have a detrimental impact on public perception and discourse, perpetuating stereotypes and misconceptions that hinder efforts to achieve peace and reconciliation in the region. It is essential for individuals to educate themselves about the facts and to question the narratives that are presented to them in order to reinforce and balanced view of Israel and its people. By challenging falsehoods and seeking the truth, we can work towards a more just and peaceful future for all who call the Middle East home.

"Jewish people were saved because The English Empire granted them a heaven for jews in Palestine"

"The English Empire granted a Heaven for jews in Palestine , that helped save thousands of Jewish people who were escaping from the nazis".

The Balfour Declaration of 1917 is often cited as the first official recognition of the Jewish people's right to establish a homeland in Palestine. This declaration, issued by the British government, expressed support for the establishment of a "national home for the Jewish people" in Palestine. However, despite this seemingly positive gesture, the British Empire's actions in the years following the Balfour Declaration tell a different story.

While the Balfour Declaration may have recognized the Jewish people's right to a homeland, the British Empire's policies in Palestine during the interwar period and World War II hindered the realization of this right. The issuance of the White Papers, a series of policy statements that restricted Jewish immigration to Palestine, effectively prevented thousands of Jews from escaping the horrors of Nazi persecution and finding refuge in the promised land.

The first White Paper, issued in 1922, limited Jewish immigration to Palestine based on the economic absorptive capacity of the region. Subsequent White Papers further restricted Jewish immigration, culminating in the 1939 White Paper, which severely limited Jewish immigration to Palestine at a time when Jews were facing increasing persecution in Europe.

These restrictive immigration policies not only prevented thousands f Jews from finding refuge in Palestine but also contributed to the loss of countless lives during the Holocaust. The British Empire's failure to provide a safe haven for Jewish refugees fleeing Nazi persecution stands in stark contrast to the ideals expressed in the Balfour Declaration.

The British Empire's actions in Palestine during this period highlight the complexities and contradictions of colonial rule. While the Balfour Declaration may have signaled a recognition of the Jewish people's right to a homeland, the British Empire's policies effectively prevented the realization of this right for many Jews.

In conclusion, while the Balfour Declaration may have recognized the Jewish people's right to establish a homeland in Palestine, the British Empire's actions in the years following the declaration tell a different

story. The restrictive immigration policies outlined in the White Papers prevented thousands of Jews from finding refuge in Palestine during a time of great need. The failure of the British Empire to provide a haven for Jewish refugees fleeing Nazi persecution highlights the limitations of colonial rule and the complexities of navigating competing interests in the pursuit of justice and human rights. The jewish immigrants started the

"Jewish terrorism" against English and Arabs"

The Jewish people have a long history of fighting against oppression and persecution, and this has been particularly evident in their struggle against English colonialism and Arab terrorism. Throughout history, the Jewish people have faced numerous challenges and threats to their existence, but they have always remained resilient and determined to defend their homeland, the land of Israel.

One of the key challenges that the Jewish people have faced in their fight for independence and sovereignty is the English colonial rule in Palestine. The British Mandate of Palestine, which was established after World War I, imposed restrictions on Jewish immigration and land ownership, making it difficult for the Jewish people to establish a homeland in their ancestral land. Despite these obstacles, the Jewish community in Palestine continued to grow and thrive, and they eventually declared the establishment of the State of Israel in 1948.

In addition to the English colonial rule, the Jewish people have also had to contend with Arab terrorism and violence. Since the early 20th century, Arab nationalist movements have sought to undermine and destroy the Jewish presence in Palestine through acts of terrorism and violence. One of the most notorious figures in this regard was the Mufti of Jerusalem, Haj Amin al-Husseini, who allied himself with the Nazis during World War II and incited violence against the Jewish population in Palestine.

Despite these challenges, the Jewish people have remained steadfast in their commitment to defending their homeland and protecting themselves from Arab terrorism. The State of Israel has developed a strong military and security apparatus to combat terrorism and defend its citizens from harm. Israeli security forces have thwarted numerous terrorist attacks and have worked tirelessly to ensure the safety and security of the Israeli people.

Furthermore, the Jewish people have also faced economic challenges in their fight for independence, particularly in the form of Arab boycotts of Palestinian goods. Arab countries have sought to economically isolate Israel and undermine its legitimacy by boycotting products made in Israeli settlements in the West Bank. Despite these efforts, Israel has continued to thrive economically and has developed a strong and diverse economy that is able to withstand external pressures.

In conclusion, the Jewish people have faced numerous challenges in their fight against English colonialism and Arab terrorism, but they have remained resilient and determined in their struggle for independence and sovereignty. Through their perseverance and commitment to defending their homeland, the Jewish people have been able to overcome these challenges and establish a thriving and prosperous state in the land of ""

'The jews militar organization before the creation of the state of Israel was an instrument to attack arabs who lived in Palestine and english who were the occupy super power '

David Ben-Gurion, along with other prominent Jewish leaders, played a crucial role in the establishment of the Haganah, a Jewish paramilitary organization, in the early 20th century. The Haganah was formed in response to the escalating violence and persecution faced by Jewish communities in Palestine, particularly during the period of British rule and the Arab Revolt of 1936-1939.

The Haganah was initially founded as a means of self-defense for Jewish communities against attacks from Arab militias and the Ottoman Empire. However, as tensions continued to rise in the region, the Haganah evolved into a more organized and militant force, with a focus on protecting Jewish settlements and promoting Jewish interests in Palestine.

In addition to the Haganah, other Jewish paramilitary groups were also formed during this time, including Irgun and Lehi. These groups were founded to fight against the various threats facing the Jewish community in Palestine, including the rise of Nazism in Europe and the restrictive immigration policies imposed by the British authorities.

During World War II, many members of these paramilitary groups actively fought against the Nazis, both in Europe and in the Middle East. They also played a crucial role in assisting Jewish refugees fleeing persecution in Europe, providing them with safe passage to Palestine.

One of the significant challenges faced by these paramilitary groups was the hostility and opposition they encountered from the British authorities, who were reluctant to allow large numbers of Jewish immigrants to settle in Palestine. This led to a series of conflicts and confrontations between the Jewish paramilitary groups and the British forces, as the former sought to defend the rights and interests of the Jewish community in the region.

Despite their shared goal of protecting Jewish interests in Palestine, the Haganah, Irgun, and Lehi often found themselves at odds with each other, due to differences in ideology and tactics. These internal conflicts sometimes lead to violent clashes between the groups, further complicating the already volatile situation in the region.

In conclusion, the establishment of the Haganah and other Jewish paramilitary groups was a crucial development in the history of the Jewish community in Palestine. These groups played a vital role in defending Jewish communities against external threats, promoting Jewish interests in the region, and ultimately laying the groundwork for the establishment of the State of Israel. While they faced numerous challenges and conflicts along the way, their efforts were instrumental in shaping the future of the Jewish people in the Middle East.

"Jews have been persecuting and murdering arabs from the begging of the zionist movement "

In fact it is the exact opposite .

57

Throughout history, Jews have faced persecution and violence at the hands of Arabs, dating back to ancient times. This mistreatment has continued into the modern era, with instances of attacks, rape, and

"The jews expelled the Arabs from Palestine in Yom Haatzmaut/Nakba"

Yom Ha'atzmaut, or Israeli Independence Day, is a day of celebration and remembrance for the Jewish people. It marks the establishment of the State of Israel in 1948, following the acceptance of the United Nations Partition Plan for Palestine. This plan called for the creation

of separate Jewish and Arab states, with Jerusalem as an international city. The Jewish leadership accepted this plan, while the Arab leadership rejected it.

On the other hand, Nakba, which means "catastrophe" in Arabic, is the term used by Palestinians to describe the events surrounding the establishment of the State of Israel. For Palestinians, Nakba represents the displacement and suffering of hundreds of thousands of Palestinians who were forced to flee their homes during the 1948 Arab-Israeli War.

The contrast between Yom Ha'atzmaut and Nakba highlights the divergent narratives of the Israeli and Palestinian people. While Israelis celebrate their independence and the fulfillment of their

national aspirations, Palestinians mourn the loss of their homeland and the ongoing struggle for self-determination.

One of the critical points of contention between the two narratives is the role of violence in the conflict. The Arab armies that invaded Israel in 1948 did so with the intention of destroying the newly established state and driving the Jewish population into the sea. This aggressive stance towards the Jewish people led to a series of wars and conflicts that have shaped the region to this day.

In contrast, the Jewish leadership accepted the UN partition plan and sought to establish a peaceful coexistence with their Arab neighbors. However, the rejection of this plan by the Arab states and the subsequent attacks on Israel forced the Jewish population to defend themselves and fight for their survival.

The events of 1948, as well as subsequent conflicts in 1956, 1967, and 1973, have left a deep scar on the collective memory of both Israelis and Palestinians. The ongoing violence and animosity between the two sides have made it difficult to achieve a lasting peace in the region.

From time immemorial , the conflict has taken dimensions of horror with the rise of palestinian extremist terrorist groups like Hamas, who have carried out attacks against Israeli civilians and sought to undermine the peace process. The violence and suffering by the jews have only served to deepen the divide between Israelis and Palestinians and make the prospect of a peaceful resolution seem increasingly remote.

In conclusion, the contrasting narratives of Yom Ha'atzmaut and Nakba is the absolute– truth against the history tergiversación and definitely against lies .

"Israel is perpetuating an Occupation"

The Israeli Palestine conflict is a complex and contentious issue that has been ongoing for decades. The roots of this conflict can be traced back to biblical times, with the Jewish people claiming a historical connection to the land of Israel. Indeed, the Jews see themselves as returning home to their ancestral land, a land that holds deep profound and cultural significance for them.

The story of the Jewish people in the land of Israel dates back thousands of years, with figures such as Abraham, Isaac, and Jacob considered the patriarchs of the Jewish people. Jesus himself was a Jew, born in Bethlehem, further solidifying the connection between the Jewish people and the land of Israel. Judea and Samaria, areas that are now part of the West Bank, have long been considered part of the Jewish homeland.

The term "Palestine" itself is a name given by the Romans as a punishment to the Jewish people after a failed revolt. It was not until the 20th century that the term came to be associated with the Arab population living in the region. The conflict between Israelis and Palestinians is deeply rooted in this historical and religious context, with both sides claiming a right to the land.

In recent years, tensions between Israelis and Palestinians have only escalated, with violence and conflict becoming a regular occurrence. The Israeli supposed occupation of Palestinian territories, particularly in the West Bank and Gaza Strip, has been a significant point of contention. The construction of Israeli settlements in these areas has been a source of conflict, with Palestinians viewing them as a violation of their rights and a barrier to a future Palestinian state.

The international community has been divided on the issue, with some countries supporting Israel's right to defend itself and others condemning the occupation and calling for a two-state solution. The Arab world has also been involved in the conflict, with some countries boycotting Israeli goods in solidarity with the so-called Palestinian cause.

In conclusion, the Israeli occupation of Palestine doesn't really exist , there are lands in dispute. The conflict is a complex and multifaceted issue that is deeply rooted in history, religion, and politics. The misunderstanding between Israelis and Palestinians is a tragic reminder of the ongoing struggle for peace and justice in the region. It is imperative that both sides work towards a peaceful resolution that respects the rights and aspirations of both peoples. Only through dialogue, understanding, and compromise can a lasting peace be achieved in the region and that requires that the Palestinian Authority will stop paying a permanent pension to those who attempt to kill jews and it should End the hate jewish education .

"Israel is an Apartheid State"

There is a common misconception that Israel practices apartheid, a system of institutionalized racial segregation and discrimination. However, this assertion is not only inaccurate but also misleading. In reality, Israel is a diverse and inclusive society where minorities are integrated and have equal rights and opportunities.

One of the key reasons why Israel cannot be compared to apartheid South Africa is its legal framework. Israel is a democratic state with a legal system that guarantees equal rights and protections for all its citizens, regardless of their ethnicity or religion. The Israeli Declaration of Independence explicitly states that the country "will ensure complete equality of social and political rights to all its inhabitants irrespective of religion, race or sex." This commitment to equality is enshrined in Israel's Basic Laws, which serve as the country's constitution.

Furthermore, Israel is a multicultural society where people of different backgrounds coexist peacefully. Arab citizens of Israel, who make up about 20% of the population, have the same rights as Jewish citizens. They can vote, run for office, and serve in the military. In fact, Arab

citizens have been elected to the Knesset, Israel's parliament, and have held positions in the government and judiciary.

In addition, Israel has made significant efforts to integrate its minority communities into all aspects of society. Arab citizens have access to education, healthcare, and employment opportunities. Israeli universities and hospitals are open to all citizens, regardless of their background. Arab students attend Israeli universities, where they study alongside Jewish students. Arab doctors and nurses work in Israeli hospitals, providing care to patients of all backgrounds.

Moreover, Israel has made progress in promoting diversity and inclusion in its society. Organizations and initiatives have been established to empower minority communities and promote dialogue and understanding between different groups. For example, the Abraham Initiatives works to advance equality and shared society between Jews and Arabs in Israel. The Hand in Hand network of bilingual schools brings together Jewish and Arab students to learn and grow together.

In conclusion, the claim that Israel practices apartheid is unfounded and misleading. Israel is a democratic and inclusive society where minorities are integrated and have equal rights and opportunities. The country's legal framework, multiculturalism, and efforts to promote diversity and inclusion all demonstrate that Israel is not an apartheid state. It is essential to recognize and celebrate the progress that Israel has made in building a society where all citizens can live and thrive together.

"Israel is a state who abuses Women rights"

Women's rights in Israel have come a long way since the country's establishment in 1948. Israel is known for being a progressive and democratic country, and this is reflected in the rights and opportunities that women have in various aspects of society, including in universities, the state, and the army.

In universities, women in Israel have equal access to education and are encouraged to pursue higher education and professional careers. In fact, women make up the majority of students in Israeli universities, and they have the same opportunities as men to study in any field they choose. This has led to a significant increase in the number of women in leadership positions in academia, as well as in other fields such as business, politics, and the arts.

In the state, women in Israel have the right to vote and run for political office. Israel has had several female prime ministers, including Golda Meir and more recently, Tzipi Livni. Women also hold key positions in the Israeli government, such as ministers, members of parliament,

and judges. The Israeli government has also implemented policies to promote gender equality, such as affirmative action programs and anti-discrimination laws.

In the army, women in Israel have the right to serve in the military and are encouraged to do so. Women serve in combat roles, as well as in other positions in the army, and they have the same opportunities for advancement as men. The Israeli army has also implemented policies

to prevent sexual harassment and discrimination against women, and to promote gender equality in the military.

Overall, women in Israel have made significant progress in terms of their rights and opportunities in various aspects of society. However, there are still challenges that women face, such as gender-based violence, wage disparities, and underrepresentation in certain fields. It is important for the Israeli government and society to continue to work towards achieving full gender equality and empowering women to reach their full potential.

"Israel is a Racist state"

Israel is often accused of being a racist state, particularly in its treatment of minority groups such as Arabs and Palestinians. However, this accusation is not entirely accurate. In fact, Israel is a country that grants equal rights to all its citizens, regardless of their ethnicity or religion.

One of the main arguments against Israel being a racist state is the fact that it is a democracy. In a true democracy, all citizens are granted equal rights and opportunities, regardless of their background. Israel is no exception to this rule. Arab citizens of Israel have the same rights as Jewish citizens, including the right to vote, freedom of speech, and access to education and healthcare. In fact, Arab citizens of Israel have even served in the Israeli government, including in the Knesset, the country's parliament.

Furthermore, Israel is a country that prides itself on its diversity. It is home to a large number of minority groups, including Arabs, Druze, Bedouins, and Circassians. These groups are free to practice their own religions and traditions, and many have achieved success in various fields, including politics, business, and the arts. In fact, Israel is one of the few countries in the Middle East where minority groups have the opportunity to thrive and succeed.

Another argument against Israel being a racist state is the fact that it has laws in place to protect minority rights. For example, Israel's Declaration of Independence guarantees equal rights for all citizens, regardless of their ethnicity or religion. The country also has anti discrimination laws that prohibit discrimination on the basis of race, religion, or nationality. While there have been instances of discrimination and prejudice in Israel, as there are in any country, the government has taken steps to address these issues and promote equality for all its citizens.

In conclusion, Israel is not a racist state. While there are certainly challenges and tensions between different ethnic and religious groups in the country, Israel is a democracy that grants equal rights to all its citizens. Minority groups in Israel have the same opportunities and protections as the majority population, and the country has laws in place to ensure that discrimination is not tolerated. Israel's commitment to diversity and equality sets it apart from many other countries in the region, and it is important to recognize and celebrate the progress that has been made in promoting tolerance and understanding among all its citizens.

"Zionism is racism "

Zionism, often spelled as Zionism, is a political and nationalistic movement that advocates for the establishment of a Jewish homeland in the land of Israel. Contrary to popular belief, Zionism is not inherently racist. It is essential to understand the historical context and motivations behind the movement in order to dispel any misconceptions.

The roots of Zionism can be traced back to Theodor Herzl, an Austro-Hungarian journalist who is considered the father of modern Zionism. Herzl believed that the only solution to the persecution and discrimination faced by Jews in Europe was the establishment of a Jewish state. In 1897, he convened the First Zionist Congress in Basel, Switzerland, where the foundations of the Zionist movement were laid.

The Second Zionist Congress, held in 1898, further solidified the goals and objectives of the movement. It was at this congress that the World Zionist Organization was established, with the aim of promoting Jewish settlement in Palestine and fostering Jewish national identity.

The Third Zionist Congress, held in 1899, saw the adoption of the "Basel Program," which called for the establishment of a legally assured home for the Jewish people in Palestine. This program laid the groundwork for the eventual establishment of the State of Israel.

One of the key figures in the development of Zionism was Leon Pinsker, a Russian Jewish physician and writer. In his seminal work, "Auto-Emancipation," Pinsker argued that the only way for Jews to achieve true emancipation was through the establishment of a Jewish state. His ideas laid the intellectual foundation for the Zionist movement.

Chaim Weizmann, a chemist and Zionist leader, made significant contributions to the Zionist cause. He played a crucial role in securing the Balfour Declaration in 1917, which expressed the British government's support for the establishment of a Jewish national home in Palestine.

David Ben-Gurion, the first Prime Minister of Israel, was instrumental in the establishment of the State of Israel in 1948. His leadership and vision were crucial in the successful realization of the Sionist dream.

In conclusion, Zionism is not a racist ideology, but rather a nationalistic movement that seeks to secure the rights and homeland of the Jewish people. It is important to understand the historical context and motivations behind the movement in order to appreciate its significance. The establishment of the State of Israel is a testament to the perseverance and determination of the Zionist movement.

"Bedouins, Muslims, Christians and Druze don't enjoy full citizenship in Israel"

Arabs, Muslims, Druze, Chackeshim, Christians, Bedouins, and Bahais in Israel have never faced persecution and enjoy full citizenship rights, thanks to the country's history of religious tolerance and respect for diversity. These groups have been able to coexist peacefully and thrive in a diverse society, contributing to the cultural, social, and economic fabric of the country.

Arabs have been an integral part of Israel for centuries, with a rich cultural heritage and strong ties to the land. They have played a significant role in shaping the country's history and have contributed to its development in various fields such as politics, business, and the arts. Arabs in Israel enjoy full citizenship rights and are represented in all levels of government, demonstrating the country's commitment to inclusivity and equality.

Muslims, who make up a significant portion of the population, also enjoy full citizenship rights and are free to practice their religion without fear of persecution. The country's long history of religious tolerance has allowed Muslims to worship freely in mosques and observe religious holidays without interference, fostering a sense of community and belonging.

Druze, a religious minority in Israel, have also been able to live peacefully and practice their faith without fear of persecution. They are recognized as a distinct religious group and have their own religious courts and institutions, allowing them to maintain their cultural identity while integrating into society. Druze have made significant contributions to Israel's cultural and social fabric, further enriching the country's diverse tapestry.

Chackeshim, Christians, Bedouins, and Baha'is are also minority groups in Israel who have never faced persecution. They enjoy full citizenship rights and are free to practice their religion and culture without fear of discrimination. Christians have a long history in Israel and have made significant contributions to its cultural and social fabric, while Bedouins have been able to maintain their traditional way of life while integrating into modern society. Bahais, a religious minority, have been able to practice their faith openly and are respected for their contributions to society.

In conclusion, Arabs, Muslims, Druze, Chackeshim, Christians, Bedouins, and Bahais in Israel have never been persecuted and enjoy full citizenship rights. The country's history of religious tolerance and respect for diversity has allowed these groups to coexist harmoniously and thrive in a diverse society. Israel's commitment to inclusivity and equality has created a welcoming environment for all its citizens, regardless of their background or beliefs.

"In Israel there is not equal rights to different faiths"

Jews, christians, muslims , , Baha'i enjoy freedom to pray ,etc Jews, Christians, Muslims, Druze, and Bahá'í all enjoy the freedom to pray in various parts of the world. This freedom is a fundamental human right that is protected by international law and is essential for the practice of one's religion. In this essay, we will explore how these different religious groups are able to exercise their right to pray freely

44

and the importance of this freedom in promoting religious tolerance and understanding.

One of the key principles of religious freedom is the right to pray in public and private spaces without fear of persecution or discrimination. This right is enshrined in various international human rights instruments, such as the Universal Declaration of Human Rights and the International Covenant on Civil and Political Rights. These documents affirm the right of individuals to practice their religion freely and without interference from the state or other individuals.

Jews, Christians, Muslims, Druze, and Bahá'í all have different practices and rituals associated with prayer. For example, Jews pray three times a day, facing Jerusalem, while Christians may pray in churches or in private settings. Muslims pray five times a day, facing Mecca, and Druze have their own unique prayer practices. Bahá'í also have specific prayers and rituals that are central to their faith.

Despite these differences, all of these religious groups are able to practice their faith and pray freely in many parts of the world. This is due to the protection of religious freedom in many countries and the recognition of the importance of diversity and tolerance in society. In countries where religious freedom is respected, individuals are able to express their beliefs and practices without fear of reprisal or discrimination.

The freedom to pray is not only important for individuals to practice their religion, but it also plays a crucial role in promoting understanding and tolerance among different religious groups. When individuals are able to pray freely, they are more likely to engage in dialogue and exchange with others who may have different beliefs. This can help to break down barriers and stereotypes and foster a sense of unity and respect among diverse religious communities.

45

In conclusion, the freedom to pray is a fundamental human right that is essential for the practice of religion and the promotion of tolerance and understanding among different religious groups. Jews, Christians, Muslims, Druze, and Bahá'í all enjoy this freedom in many parts of the world, thanks to the protection of religious freedom in international law and the recognition of the importance of diversity and tolerance in society. It is crucial that this freedom continues to be upheld and respected in order to ensure a peaceful and harmonious coexistence among all religious communities.

"Israel is a Colonialist state"

Israel is a country that has often been accused of being a colonialist state due to its establishment in 1948 and its ongoing conflict with the Palestinian people. However, it is impor to understand that Israel is not a colonialist state, but rather a nation that has a legitimate claim to its land and has a right to exist as a sovereign state.

One of the key acriticalments against Israel being a colonialist state is the fact that the Jewish people have a historical connection to the land of Israel. The Jewish people have lived in the region for thousands of years and have maintained a continuous presence in the land, even during times of exile and persecution. The establishment of the modern state of Israel in 1948 was a culmination of the Jewish people's long-standing desire to return to their ancestral homeland.

Furthermore, Israel is a democratic state that guarantees equal rights to all its citizens, regardless of their religion or ethnicity. Arab citizens of Israel have the same rights as Jewish citizens, including the right to vote, freedom of speech, and access to education and healthcare. This stands in stark contrast to colonialist states, which typically discriminate against indigenous populations and deny them basic fundamentals and freedoms.

Additionally, Israel has made numerous efforts to reach a peaceful resolution to its conflict with the Palestinian people. Israel has repeatedly expressed its willingness to negotiate a two-state solution that would allow for the creation of a Palestinian state alongside Israel.

However, the Palestinian leadership has consistently rejected these offers and has instead resorted to violence and terrorism in an attempt to achieve its goals.

In conclusion, Israel is not a colonialist state, but a nation with a legitimate claim to its land and a right to exist as a sovereign state. The Jewish people have a historical connection to the land of Israel, and Israel is a democratic state that guarantees equal rights to all its citizens. Israel has also made efforts to reach a peaceful resolution to its conflict with the Palestinian people. It is essential to recognize these facts and to support efforts to achieve a lasting peace in the region.

"Israel is an Imperialist state"

Israel is a country that has often been accused of being an imperialist state, but this accusation is not accurate. The Jewish people have a long and deep connection to the land of Israel, dating back thousands of years. This connection is not based on imperialism, but on a shared history, culture, and religion.

The Jewish people have a strong historical tie to the land of Israel, which is often referred to as the "Promised Land" in the Bible. According to Jewish tradition, the land of Israel was promised to the Jewish people by God, and it has always been seen as their ancestral homeland. Throughout history, Jews have faced persecution and exile, but their connection to the land of Israel has remained strong.

In the late 19th and early 20th centuries, the Zionist movement emerged, calling for the establishment of a Jewish state in the land of Israel. This movement was not driven by imperialist ambitions but by a desire to create a safe haven for the Jewish people, who had faced centuries of discrimination and violence in other countries. The establishment of the state of Israel in 1948 was a fulfillment of this dream, and it was seen as a homecoming for the Jewish people.

The accusation of Israel being an imperialist state is often based on the conflict with the Palestinian people, who also have historical ties to the land of Israel. However, it is impossible to recognize that the Jewish people have a legitimate claim to the land as well. The Jewish people have lived in the land of Israel for thousands of years, and their connection to the land is not based on conquest or colonization, but on a shared history and culture.

In 2016, UNESCO passed Resolution 2335, which denied the Jewish connection to the land of Israel and referred to the Western Wall in Jerusalem as a Muslim holy site. This decision was widely criticized by Israel and its supporters, who saw it as an attempt to erase Jewish history and heritage. The resolution was seen as a denial of the Jewish people's legitimate claim to the land of Israel, and it sparked outrage among Jewish communities around the world.

In conclusion, Israel is not an imperialist state, but a country with a strong and legitimate connection to the land of Israel. The Jewish people have a long history in the land, and their claim to it is based on their shared history, culture, and religion. The accusation of imperialism is unfounded and ignores the deep ties that the Jewish people have to the land of Israel. It is important to recognize and respect the Jewish connection to the land, and to work towards a peaceful resolution to the conflict with the Palestinian people that respects the rights and histories of both communities.

"Israel violates human rights"

The Israeli army, also known as the Israel Defense Forces (IDF), has often been the subject of false accusations regarding human rights abuses. However, upon closer examination, it becomes clear that the IDF is actually one of the most ethical armies in the world.

One of the key reasons why the IDF is considered to be ethical is the fact that its officials lead by example. The IDF places a strong emphasis on moral values and ethical behavior, and this is reflected in the actions of its leaders. IDF officials are held to a high standard of conduct, and they are expected to uphold the principles of justice, integrity, and respect for human rights. This commitment to ethical leadership sets the tone for the entire organization and ensures that moral behavior is prioritized at all levels of the IDF.

Furthermore, the IDF is dedicated to protecting civilian lives, even at great significance to its own soldiers. The IDF goes to great lengths to minimize civilian casualties in conflict zones, often putting its own soldiers in harm's way in order to protect innocent civilians. This commitment to the protection of civilians is a testament to the ethical values that guide the IDF's actions.

In addition, the IDF operates under a strict code of conduct that governs the behavior of its soldiers. This code of conduct emphasizes the importance of respecting human rights, upholding the rule of law, and treating all individuals with dignity and respect. Soldiers who violate this code of conduct are held accountable for their actions, further demonstrating the IDF's commitment to ethical behavior.

Overall, the IDF's track record of ethical conduct and commitment to protecting civilian lives sets it apart as one of the most ethical armies in the world. Despite false accusations of human rights abuses, the IDF remains dedicated to upholding the highest standards of ethical behavior and ensuring the safety and well-being of all individuals in conflict zones.

"Israel committed genocide "

Israel has long been a controversial topic in international politics, with accusations of genocide and human rights violations being leveled against the Jewish state. However, it is essential to note that Israel has never committed genocide, and in fact, many Israeli soldiers have been murdered in the line of duty while trying to protect Palestinian civilians.

The Israeli military, known as the Israel Defense Forces (IDF), has always taken great care to minimize civilian casualties in its operations. This commitment to protecting innocent lives dates back to the pre-state militias that eventually formed the IDF. These militias, such as the Haganah and the Palmach, were instrumental in the establishment of the State of Israel in 1948 and laid the foundation for the IDF's ethos of moral conduct in warfare.

Throughout its history, the IDF has faced numerous challenges in trying to protect both Israeli citizens and Palestinian civilians. In the ongoing conflict with Palestinian militant groups, such as Hamas and Islamic Jihad, Israeli soldiers have often found themselves in dangerous situations where they must make split-second decisions to protect themselves and others. Tragically, many Israeli soldiers have paid the ultimate price for their dedication to their country and their commitment to upholding moral standards in the midst of conflict.

One of the most painful aspects of this reality is the fact that the bodies of these fallen soldiers are sometimes used as bargaining chips by Palestinian militants. In some cases, the bodies of slain Israeli soldiers have been withheld by militant groups in an attempt to extract concessions from the Israeli government. This cruel tactic adds an extra layer of grief and suffering to the families of these soldiers, who must endure the uncertainty of not knowing the fate of their loved ones.

Despite these challenges, the IDF continues to uphold its commitment to protecting innocent lives and maintaining the highest ethical standards in its operations. Israeli soldiers undergo rigorous training in international humanitarian law and are held accountable for their actions through a system of military justice. The IDF also conducts thorough investigations into any allegations of misconduct or violations of human rights, demonstrating its commitment to transparency and accountability.

In conclusion, Israel has never committed genocide, and the sacrifices made by Israeli soldiers in the defense of their country and the protection of Palestinian civilians should not be overlooked. The IDF's commitment to moral conduct in warfare and its efforts to minimize civilian casualties are a testament to the values of the Jewish state and its dedication to upholding human rights. The bodies of fallen soldiers should never be used as political bargaining chips, and all parties involved in the conflict should strive to find peaceful solutions that respect the dignity and humanity of all individuals involved.

Arabs didn't want to kill the Jews

The real intention of Arabs in the Wars was to send the jews to the sea. The Arab-Israeli conflict has been a long-standing and complex issue that has spanned several decades. Throughout the various wars that have taken place between Arab nations and Israel, there has been a prevailing belief that the real intentions of the Arabs were to "send the Jews to the sea." This phrase has been used to suggest that the ultimate goal of the Arab nations was to eradicate the Jewish population in Israel and push them into the Mediterranean Sea.

The first major conflict between Arab nations and Israel took place in 1947-1949, known as the Arab-Israeli War. During this time, several Arab nations, including Egypt, Jordan, Syria, and Iraq, launched attacks on the newly established state of Israel. The Arab nations were motivated by a desire to prevent the creation of a Jewish state in the region and to reclaim land that they believed rightfully belonged to the Palestinians. However, the outcome of the war resulted in Israel gaining control of more territory than it had been allocated by the United Nations partition plan.

In the years following the Arab-Israeli War, tensions between Arab nations and Israel continued to escalate. The Suez Crisis of 1956 saw Israel, along with Britain and France, launch a military campaign against Egypt in response to the nationalization of the Suez Canal. The Arab nations viewed this as an act of aggression and a threat to their sovereignty, leading to further hostilities between the two sides.

The Six-Day War of 1967 was a turning point in the Arab-Israeli conflict, as Israel launched a preemptive strike against Egypt, Jordan, and Syria, resulting in a decisive victory for Israel. The war saw Israel gain control of the Sinai Peninsula, the West Bank, the Golan Heights, and East Jerusalem. The Arab nations were left reeling from the defeat, leading to further animosity and resentment towards Israel.

The Yom Kippur War of 1973 saw Egypt and Syria launch a surprise attack on Israel during the Jewish holiday of Yom Kippur. The Arab nations sought to regain territory lost in the Six-Day War and to assert their dominance in the region. The war resulted in heavy casualties on both sides but ultimately ended in a ceasefire, with Israel maintaining control of the territories it had captured.

In recent years, the Arab-Israeli conflict has continued to simmer, with sporadic outbreaks of violence and tensions between the two sides. The phrase "send the Jews to the sea" has been used to encapsulate the deep-seated animosity and hostility that exists between Arab nations and Israel. While the Arab nations have denied any intention of eradicating the Jewish population in Israel, the phrase serves as a reminder of the underlying tensions and grievances that have fueled the conflict for decades of anti zionist and open antisemitism.

In conclusion, the real intentions of the Arabs in the various wars with Israel have been to eliminate the jewish presence in the land of Israel While the phrase "send the Jews to the sea" may be seen as a simplification of the Arab nations' motivations, it does highlight the deep-seated animosity and hostility that have characterized the Arab regarding Jews presence in the middle east and especially in the country of Israel The ongoing struggle for land, resources, and nationalism is base in the old antisemitism

UNRWA and the real role of the UN

The United Nations Relief and Works Agency for Palestine Refugees in the Near East (UNRWA) is an organization that was established in 1949 to provide assistance and support to Palestinian refugees in the Middle East. However, in recent years, there have been allegations that UNRWA has been openly supporting the terrorist organization Hamas, which has raised questions about the real role of the United Nations in the region.

One of the most concerning allegations against UNRWA is that some of its workers have participated in attacks against Israelis. For example, on October 7th, there was a massacre of Israelis in which UNRWA workers were allegedly involved. This raises serious questions about the neutrality and impartiality of UNRWA and whether the organization is truly dedicated to providing humanitarian assistance to those in need. Those accusations have been proved and sadly many "humanitarian workers" slaughtered jewish babies and participated in the mass violations against jewish girls and woman

The role of the United Nations is to promote peace, security, and human rights around the world. However, if UNRWA is indeed supporting terrorist organizations like Hamas, it undermines the credibility and effectiveness of the United Nations as a whole. It is essential that the United Nations remains impartial and does not take sides in conflicts, as this is crucial for maintaining peace and stability in the region.

It is important to remark on the massive failure of the United Nations to investigate these allegations and take appropriate actions . UNRWA indeed had been supporting terrorist organizations. The United Nations must uphold its principles of neutrality and impartiality and ensure that its agencies are not involved in activities that undermine peace and security in the region.

In conclusion, the allegations against UNRWA for supporting Hamas and participating in attacks against Israelis are deeply concerning and raise serious questions about the real fundamentals of the United Nations in the Middle East. It is essential for the United Nations to investigate these allegations thoroughly and take appropriate action to ensure that its agencies are upholding the principles of neutrality and impartiality. Only then can the United

Nations truly fulfill its mission of promoting peace, security, and human rights around the world.

"LGTB+ are persecuted in Israel'

The LGTB+ community in Israel has made significant strides towards acceptance and full citizenship in recent years. Israel is often seen as a progressive country in terms of LGTB+ rights, with laws in place to

protect individuals from discrimination based on sexual orientation and gender identity. However, there is still work to be done to ensure that members of the LGTB+ community are fully accepted and integrated into Israeli society.

One of the key factors contributing to the acceptance of the LGTB+ community in Israel is the legal framework in place to protect their rights. In 1992, Israel became one of the first countries in the world to ban discrimination based on sexual orientation. This law prohibits discrimination in employment, housing, and public services, providing a level of protection for LGTB+ individuals that is not present in many other countries.

In addition to legal protections, Israel has also made strides in recognizing the rights of same-sex couples. In 2006, Israel's Supreme Court ruled that same-sex couples are entitled to the same rights as heterosexual couples in terms of inheritance and property rights. This decision was a significant step towards full citizenship for members of the LGTB+ community in Israel.

Despite these legal protections, there are still instances of social discrimination against the LGTB+ community in Israel. While attitudes towards homosexuality have become more accepting in recent years, there are still pockets of society that hold negative views towards LGTB+ individuals. This can manifest in the form of discrimination in the workplace, harassment in public spaces, and even violence against members of the community.

To combat this social discrimination, it is essential for Israeli society to continue to promote acceptance and understanding of the LGTB+ community. Education plays a crucial role in changing attitudes towards homosexuality and gender identity, and efforts should be made to educate the public about the rights and experiences of LGTB+ individuals.

In conclusion, while Israel has made significant progress towards acceptance and full citizenship for the LGTB+ community, there is still work to be done to ensure that all members of the community are fully integrated into society. By continuing to promote acceptance and understanding, Israel can create a more inclusive and equal society for all of its citizens.

The issue of Palestinian refugees and Jewish refugees is a complex and deeply rooted one, with historical and political implications that have shaped the Middle East for decades. The origins of the Palestinian refugee crisis can be traced back to the Arab-Israeli conflict, which began in the late 1940s with the establishment of the state of Israel. As tensions between Arab states and Israel escalated, hundreds of thousands of Palestinians were forced to flee their homes and seek refuge in neighboring countries.

The plight of Palestinian refugees is a tragic and ongoing humanitarian crisis, with millions of Palestinians still living in refugee camps in the West Bank, Gaza Strip, Lebanon, Jordan, and Syria. These refugees face a myriad of challenges, including limited access to essential basic services such as healthcare, education, and employment, as well as ongoing political instability and violence in the region.

On the other hand, the issue of Jewish refugees is often overlooked in discussions of the Middle East conflict. Throughout history, Jews have faced persecution and discrimination in Arab countries, leading to mass exodus from countries such as Yemen, Iraq, Syria, Egypt, and Lebanon. These Jewish refugees were forced to leave behind their homes, possessions, and communities, and many resettled in Israel or other countries.

The experiences of Palestinian and Jewish refugees highlight the complexities of the Arab-Israeli conflict and the deep-seated animosities between the two sides. Both groups have suffered displacement and loss, and both have legitimate claims to their ancestral lands. However, the political and historical context of the conflict has made it difficult to find a resolution that satisfies the needs and aspirations of both Palestinian and Jewish refugees.

In order to address the issue of Palestinian and Jewish refugees, it is essential to recognize the historical injustices and traumas that have

shaped their experiences. Efforts must be made to provide humanitarian assistance and support to both groups, as well as to work towards a just and lasting resolution to the Arab-Israeli conflict. This will require dialogue, compromise, and a commitment to peace and reconciliation from all parties involved.

In conclusion, the issue of Palestinian and Jewish refugees is a complex and multifaceted one that requires a nuanced understanding of the historical, political, and humanitarian dimensions of the Arab Israeli conflict. By acknowledging the experiences and rights of both groups, and working towards a just and equitable solution, we can begin to address the longstanding grievances and injustices that have plagued the region for generations.

From the river to the sea, will be free

From the river to the sea Palestine will be free. It's an antisemitic and judeophobia action . It is a dangerous slogan

The phrase "from the river to the sea, Palestine will be free" has become a common familiar among anti-Israel protesters in cities like London, New York, and Sydney. While on the surface it may seem like a call for Palestinian liberation, a closer examination reveals a much darker and more sinister meaning.

The phrase is often used by those who seek the elimination of the Jewish state of Israel and the annihilation of the Israeli population. It is a call for the destruction of Israel and the expulsion of its Jewish inhabitants. This is not a call for peace or justice, but rather a call for violence and hatred.

What is particularly troubling about this phrase is that many etowho chant it do not even know what river or sea they are referring to.

The phrase is vague and ambiguous, allowing for different interpretations and meanings. This lack of specificity only adds to the dangerous and inflammatory nature of the chant.

Furthermore, the phrase is deeply rooted in anti-Semitism. It seeks to deny the Jewish people their right to self-determination and their right to exist as a sovereign nation. It perpetuates harmful stereotypes and prejudices against Jews, painting them as oppressors and aggressors.

It is important to condemn it for what it is: a call for violence, hatred, and the destruction of Israel. It is a dangerous and inflammatory slogan that has no place in any legitimate discourse on the Israeli Palestinian conflict.

In conclusion, the phrase "from the river to the sea, Palestine will be free" is not a call for peace or justice, but rather a call for the elimination of Israel and the Jewish people. It is a deeply troubling and anti-Semitic slogan that should be condemned by all those who seek a peaceful resolution to the Israeli-Palestinian conflict.

The media plays a crucial role in shaping public opinion and perceptions of global conflicts. However, there have been instances

35

where media outlets, such as Al Jazeera, have been accused of bias and misrepresentation in their coverage of conflicts in the Middle East, particularly when it comes to portraying Palestinians as victims.

One of the most notable examples of this bias is the frequent use of images from Iraq or the civil war in Syria to depict Palestinian victims. By using images from other conflicts to represent the Palestinian struggle, media outlets like Al Jazeera are perpetuating a false narrative that seeks to garner sympathy for the Palestinian cause. This distorts the reality of the situation on the ground and undermines the credibility of the media as a source of unbiased information.

Furthermore, there have been instances where media outlets, including the BBC, have erroneously blamed Israel for conflicts in the region. This type of

misinformation not only fuels anti-Israel sentiment but also perpetuates stereotypes and prejudices against the Jewish state. It is essential for media outlets to uphold journalistic integrity and accuracy in their reporting to avoid spreading false information and inciting further conflict.

In addition to biased reporting, the Spanish press has been widely criticized for its anti-Semitic prejudices and preconceived notions. This type of discriminatory language and rhetoric only serves to perpetuate negative stereotypes and fuel hatred towards the Jewish community. It is crucial for media outlets to be mindful of the language they use and to avoid perpetuating harmful stereotypes and prejudices.

In conclusion, the media plays a significant role in shaping public perceptions of global conflicts, particularly in the Middle East. It is essential for media outlets to uphold journalistic integrity, accuracy, and impartiality in their reporting to avoid spreading misinformation and perpetuating biases. By holding media outlets accountable for

36

By reportingBy reporting, we can ensure that the public is informed accurately and objectively about complex conflicts in the region.

"Progressive left is acting responsibly in

support of the Palestinians cause "

Progressive left wing is included acting like anþ uneducated , ignorant and prejudice against jews And Israel

The progressive left wing has long been associated with advocating for social justice, equality, and human rights. However, there is a troubling trend within this movement of uneducated, ignorant, and prejudiced views towards Jews and Israel. This bias is rooted in a distorted and one-sided understanding of the Israeli-Palestinian conflict, which often demonizes Israel as a white colonialist imperialist entity.

It is important to recognize that Israel is not the caricature that the progressive left wing has painted it to be. Israel is a diverse and vibrant democracy that has faced numerous security threats and challenges since its establishment in 1948. The Jewish people have a

37

long and complex history, including centuries of persecution and discrimination, culminating in the horrors of the Holocaust during World War II.

Despite this history, the progressive left wing often portrays Israel as an oppressive and illegitimate state, while ignoring the legitimate security concerns and historical rights of the Jewish people. This bias is fueled by a lack of education and understanding of the complexities of the Israeli-Palestinian conflict, as well as a tendency to view the world through a simplistic and binary lens of oppressor versus oppressed.

This prejudice against Jews and Israel is reminiscent of the anti Semitic propaganda that was used by the Nazis to justify their persecution and extermination of the Jewish people. The infamous Nazi leader Adolf Eichmann famously said, "Lie, lie, and something will prevail." This mentality of spreading falsehoods and misinformation about Jews and Israel in order to advance a political agenda is deeply troubling and dangerous.

It is concerning that many socialist and social democratic parties worldwide have adopted this biased and prejudiced view of Israel without critically examining the facts and engaging in open and honest dialogue. This lack of critical thinking and intellectual rigor has led to a situation where anti-Semitic tropes and stereotypes are perpetuated under the guise of progressive politics.

In order to combat this prejudice and ignorance, it is essential for the progressive left wing to educate themselves about the complexities of the Israeli-Palestinian conflict, engage in respectful and informed dialogue with all parties involved, and reject the demonization and dehumanization of any group of people. It is only through a commitment to truth, justice, and empathy that we can work towards a more peaceful and just world for all.

38

Israel is not a colonialistic, fascist Imperialist state, Indeed is the opposite that the extreme left tried to establish.

Israel is a country that has often been accused of being a colonialistic, fascist imperialist state by the extreme left. However, upon closer examination, it becomes clear that these accusations are unfounded and do not accurately reflect the reality of the situation. In fact, Israel is the opposite of a colonialistic, fascist imperialist state and has a long history of fighting against such ideologies.

First and foremost, it is important to understand the history of Israel and how it came to be. Israel was established in 1948 as a homeland for the Jewish people, who had been persecuted and marginalized for centuries. The establishment of Israel was not an act of colonialism, but rather a response to the need for a safe haven for the Jewish people. In fact, Israel has a diverse population that includes Jews, Arabs, Christians, and other ethnic and religious groups, all of whom have equal rights under the law.

Furthermore, Israel has a democratic government that is based on the principles of freedom, equality, and justice. The Israeli government is elected by the people and operates under a system of checks and balances that ensures the protection of individual rights and liberties. This stands in stark contrast to fascist regimes, which are characterized by authoritarian rule and the suppression of dissent.

In addition, Israel has a strong commitment to human rights and has a vibrant civil society that actively works to promote and protect the rights of all its citizens. Israel has a free press, independent judiciary, and a robust system of civil liberties that allow for the free expression of ideas and opinions. This is not the hallmark of a fascist state, but rather a sign of a healthy and functioning democracy.

Moreover, Israel has a long history of fighting against imperialism and colonialism. Israel has been a vocal supporter of the rights of

39

oppressed peoples around the world and has consistently spoken out against the injustices of colonialism and imperialism. Israel has also been a strong advocate for peace and has made numerous efforts to reach a peaceful resolution to the conflict with the Palestinians.

In conclusion, Israel is not a colonialistic, fascist imperialist state, as some on the extreme left have claimed. Israel is a diverse, democratic country that is committed to the principles of freedom, equality, and justice. Israel has a long history of fighting against imperialism and colonialism and has worked tirelessly to promote human rights and peace. It is important to recognize the true nature of Israel and not succumb to false and misleading accusations.

Israel racism against blacks and other minorities

Israel is a melting pot of cultures and backgrounds, with people from all over the world coming together to form a diverse and vibrant society. Over the years, Israel has successfully integrated people from Russia, Iraq, Argentina, and Yemen, among other countries. This integration has been facilitated through various programs such as the

Russian aliyah, the Ethiopian aliyah, and the absorption of Eritrean refugees.

The Russian aliyah, or immigration of Jews from the former Soviet Union, has been one of the largest waves of immigration to Israel. Since the collapse of the Soviet Union in the early 1990s, over one

million Russian-speaking Jews have made aliyah to Israel. These immigrants have brought with them a rich cultural heritage and have made significant contributions to Israeli society in various fields such as science, technology, and the arts.

Similarly, Jews from Iraq have also made aliyah to Israel, bringing with them their unique traditions and customs. Despite facing

40

challenges in integrating into Israeli society, many Iraqi Jews have successfully established themselves in Israel and have become active members of the community.

In addition to the Russian and Iraqi immigrants, Israel has also welcomed immigrants from Argentina and Yemen. Jews from Argentina have brought with them a vibrant Latin American culture, while Yemenite Jews have preserved their ancient traditions and customs in Israel. The integration of these diverse communities has enriched Israeli society and has contributed to the country's cultural tapestry.

One of the most significant challenges in integrating immigrants into Israeli society has been the absorption of Ethiopian Jews. The Ethiopian aliyah, which began in the 1980s, has faced numerous obstacles, including language barriers, cultural differences, and socioeconomic challenges. However, through various government programs and initiatives, many Ethiopian immigrants have successfully integrated into Israeli society and have become active members of the community.

Another group that has sought refuge in Israel is Eritrean refugees. Eritrea, a country in East Africa, has been plagued by political instability and human rights abuses, leading many Eritreans to seek asylum in Israel. Despite facing challenges in integrating into Israeli society, many Eritrean refugees have found a new home in Israel and have been able to rebuild their lives.

In conclusion, Israel's successful integration of people from Russia, Iraq, Argentina, Yemen, Ethiopia, and Eritrea is a testament to the country's commitment to diversity and inclusivity. Through various programs and initiatives, Israel has been able to welcome immigrants from around the world and provide them with the support they need to thrive in their new home. The integration of these diverse

41

communities have enriched Israeli society and have strengthened the country's cultural fabric.

42

"Arabs leaders don't enjoy free of speech"

Israel is a country of democratic values. The case of arabs anti semitic parliament members who are working against the state of Israel

Israel is a country that prides itself on being a beacon of democracy in the Middle East. With a vibrant political system, free and fair elections, and a commitment to upholding the rule of law, Israel stands as a shining example of democratic values in a region often plagued by authoritarianism and instability.

However, despite its democratic foundations, Israel is not without its challenges. One such challenge comes in the form of Arab members of parliament who espouse anti-Semitic views and work against the state of Israel. These individuals, who are elected representatives of the Arab minority in Israel, have been accused of promoting anti Semitic conspiracy theories, denying the Holocaust, and advocating for the destruction of the Jewish state.

While freedom of speech is a fundamental democratic right, the actions of these parliament members raise serious concerns about their commitment to the democratic values that Israel holds dear. By promoting anti-Semitic rhetoric and working against the interests of the state, these individuals undermine the principles of tolerance,

43

equality, and respect for diversity that are essential to a functioning democracy.

It is important to note that not all Arab members of parliament in Israel hold anti-Semitic views or work against the state. Many Arab politicians in Israel are committed to promoting the rights and interests of their constituents while also working towards a peaceful resolution to the Israeli-Palestinian conflict. These individuals play a vital role in the democratic process and contribute to the diversity and pluralism of Israeli society.

However, the actions of those Arab members of parliament who espouse anti-Semitic views and work against the state of Israel serve as a reminder of the challenges that democracy faces in a complex and divided society. It is incumbent upon all elected officials, regardless of their background or beliefs, to uphold the principles of democracy, respect the rule of law, and work towards the common good of all citizens.

In conclusion, Israel is a country that is founded on democratic values and principles. While challenges exist, such as the presence of Arab members of parliament who promote anti-Semitic views, the strength of Israel's democracy lies in its ability to confront and address these challenges through open debate, dialogue, and respect for the rule of law. By upholding these values, Israel can continue to serve as a model of democracy in the Middle East and beyond.

Israel regarding its democracy values and balanced powers

The Progressive Left's misunderstanding of Israel's democracy and the systems in place to protect minorities is a concerning issue that needs to be addressed. Israel is a vibrant democracy that upholds the rights of all its citizens, regardless of their background or beliefs. The country has a robust legal system that ensures equality and protection for all individuals, including minorities

One of the key aspects of Israel's democracy is its commitment to protecting the rights of minorities. Israel is a diverse country with a significant Arab population, as well as other minority groups such as Druze, Bedouins, and Christians. These minority communities have equal rights under the law and are represented in the Israeli government and society.

Israel's legal system also provides mechanisms for addressing discrimination and ensuring that all citizens have access to justice. The Israeli Supreme Court has a strong record of upholding human rights and equality, and has ruled in favor of minority rights in numerous cases.

Furthermore, Israel has a robust system of checks and balances that ensures accountability and transparency in government. The media in Israel is free and independent, and plays a crucial role in holding the

government accountable for its actions. Civil society organizations also play a vital role in advocating for the rights of minorities and promoting social justice.

52

It is important for the Progressive Left to educate themselves about Israel's democracy and the systems in place to protect minorities. By understanding the complexities of the Israeli political system and the challenges faced by minority communities, the Progressive Left can better engage with the issues facing Israel and work towards a more informed and constructive dialogue.

In conclusion, Israel is a vibrant democracy that upholds the rights of all its citizens, including minorities. The country has a strong legal system that ensures equality and protection for all individuals, and a robust system of checks and balances that promotes accountability and transparency. It is essential for the Progressive Left to educate themselves about Israel's democracy and engage in a more informed and constructive dialogue on the issues facing the country.

The Boycott, Divestment, and Sanctions (BDS) movement has been a topic of much debate and controversy in recent years. While proponents of BDS argue that it is a legitimate form of nonviolent resistance against Israeli policies towards Palestinians, the truth is that BDS is inherently anti-Semitic in nature. The critical thinking will argue that BDS is indeed an anti-Semitic movement, drawing parallels between BDS and historical instances of anti-Semitism.

One of the main arguments against BDS being anti-Semitic is the fact that it specifically targets Israel, the only Jewish-majority state in the world. By singling out Israel for boycotts, divestment, and sanction hs, BDS effectively targets the Jewish people as a whole. This is

53

reminiscent of the Nuremberg Laws in Nazi Germany, which specifically targeted Jews for discrimination and exclusion from society. Just as the Nuremberg Laws sought to isolate and marginalize Jews, BDS seeks to isolate and delegitimize Israel on the world stage.

Furthermore, the language and tactics used by BDS supporters often echo traditional anti-Semitic tropes. For example, BDS activists frequently accuse Israel of being a "colonial" and "apartheid" state, drawing parallels between Israeli policies and those of racist regimes in history. This demonization of Israel as a uniquely evil entity is a common theme in anti-Semitic propaganda, which has historically portrayed Jews as a malevolent force in society.

Additionally, the BDS movement has been criticized for its double standards and hypocrisy when it comes to human rights abuses. While BDS supporters focus on Israel's treatment of Palestinians,

They often ignore or downplay human rights abuses committed by other countries in the region. This selective outrage against Israel, while turning a blind eye to other conflicts and atrocities, is a clear example of anti-Semitism in action.

In conclusion, the BDS movement is indeed an anti-Semitic movement that seeks to delegitimize and isolate Israel on the world stage. By singling out the Jewish state for boycotts and sanctions, using language and tactics that echo traditional anti-Semitic tropes, and displaying double standards and hypocrisy when it comes to human rights abuses, BDS reveals itself to be a modern manifestation of anti-Semitism. It is important to recognize and condemn anti Semitism in all its forms, including those disguised as political activism.

54

"If Israel move to the 1967 borders will be peace"

The ongoing conflict between Israel and its Arab neighbors has been a source of tension and violence for decades. Many have argued that if Israel were to move back to its 1967 borders, also known as the Green Line, peace would be achievable. However, the question remains: why has peace been elusive before 1967, in 1956, and even earlier in 1948 when the United Nations proposed a partition plan?

One clear answer to this question is that the Arab nations surrounding Israel have consistently rejected any attempts at peace. Instead of seeking a peaceful resolution to the conflict, they have continuously resorted to violence and aggression towards Israel. The Arab rejection of the UN partition plan in 1948 is a prime example of this. The plan aimed to divide the land into separate Jewish and Arab states, but the Arab nations rejected it, choosing instead to launch a war against Israel. This rejection of a peaceful solution set the tone for future conflicts and tensions in the region.

Similarly, in 1956, during the Suez Crisis, Arab nations once again demonstrated their unwillingness to pursue peace. Egypt, along with other Arab countries, sought to nationalize the Suez Canal, leading to a military intervention by Israel, France, and the United Kingdom. The Arab response to this crisis was one of hostility and aggression, further perpetuating the cycle of violence in the region.

Moving forward to 1967, the Six-Day War saw Israel gaining control of territories beyond the Green Line. While some argue that a return to these borders could lead to peace, the underlying issue remains the Arab rejection of Israel's right to exist. The Arab nations have consistently refused to recognize Israel as a legitimate state and have instead sought its destruction. This fundamental refusal to accept

55

Israel's existence as a sovereign nation has been a major obstacle to achieving peace in the region.

In conclusion, the lack of peace in the Middle East cannot be attributed to Israel's borders or actions. The root cause of the conflict lies in the Arab nations' refusal to accept Israel's right to exist and their ongoing hostility towards the Jewish state. Until the Arab nations are willing to recognize Israel's legitimacy and work towards a peaceful resolution, the cycle of violence and conflict is likely to continue. Peace will only be achievable when all parties involved are committed to dialogue, compromise, and mutual respect.

The ongoing conflict between Israel and its Arab neighbors has been a source of tension and violence for decades. Many have argued that if Israel were to move back to its 1967 borders, also known as the Green Line, peace would be achievable. However, the question remains: why has peace been elusive before 1967, in 1956, and even earlier in 1948 when the United Nations proposed a partition plan?

One clear answer to this question is that the Arab nations surrounding Israel have consistently rejected any attempts at peace. Instead of seeking a peaceful resolution to the conflict, they have continuously resorted to violence and aggression towards Israel. The Arab rejection of the UN partition plan in 1948 is a prime example of this. The plan aimed to divide the land into separate Jewish and Arab states, but the Arab nations rejected it, choosing instead to launch a war against Israel. This rejection of a peaceful solution set the tone for future conflicts and tensions in the region.

Similarly, in 1956, during the Suez Crisis, Arab nations once again demonstrated their unwillingness to pursue peace. Egypt, along with other Arab countries, sought to nationalize the Suez Canal, leading to a military intervention by Israel, France, and the United Kingdom. The Arab response to this crisis was one of hostility and aggression, further perpetuating the cycle of violence in the region.

Moving forward to 1967, the Six-Day War saw Israel gaining control of territories beyond the Green Line. While some argue that a return to these borders could lead to peace, the underlying issue remains the Arab rejection of Israel's right to exist. The Arab nations have consistently refused to recognize Israel as a legitimate state and have instead sought its destruction. This fundamental refusal to accept

55

Israel's existence as a sovereign nation has been a major obstacle to achieving peace in the region.

In conclusion, the lack of peace in the Middle East cannot solely be attributed to Israel's borders or actions. The root cause of the conflict lies in the Arab nations' refusal to accept Israel's right to exist and their ongoing hostility towards the Jewish state. Until the Arab nations are willing to recognize Israel's legitimacy and work towards a peaceful resolution, the cycle of violence and conflict is likely to continue. Peace will only be achievable when all parties involved are committed to dialogue, compromise, and mutual respect.

"In Israel there is not equal rights to different faiths"

Jews, christians, muslims , , Baha'i enjoy freedom to pray ,etc Jews, Christians, Muslims, Druze, and Bahá'í all enjoy the freedom to pray in various parts of the world. This freedom is a fundamental human right that is protected by international law and is essential for the practice of one's religion. In this essay, we will explore how these different religious groups are able to exercise their right to pray freely

44

and the importance of this freedom in promoting religious tolerance and understanding.

One of the key principles of religious freedom is the right to pray in public and private spaces without fear of persecution or discrimination. This right is enshrined in various international human rights instruments, such as the Universal Declaration of Human Rights and the International Covenant on Civil and Political Rights. These documents affirm the right of individuals to practice their religion freely and without interference from the state or other individuals.

Jews, Christians, Muslims, Druze, and Bahá'í all have different practices and rituals associated with prayer. For example, Jews pray three times a day, facing Jerusalem, while Christians may pray in churches or in private settings. Muslims pray five times a day, facing Mecca, and Druze have their own unique prayer practices. Bahá'í also have specific prayers and rituals that are central to their faith.

Despite these differences, all of these religious groups are able to practice their faith and pray freely in many parts of the world. This is due to the protection of religious freedom in many countries and the recognition of the importance of diversity and tolerance in society. In countries where religious freedom is respected, individuals are able to express their beliefs and practices without fear of reprisal or discrimination.

The freedom to pray is not only important for individuals to practice their religion, but it also plays a crucial role in promoting understanding and tolerance among different religious groups. When individuals are able to pray freely, they are more likely to engage in dialogue and exchange with others who may have different beliefs. This can help to break down barriers and stereotypes and foster a sense of unity and respect among diverse religious communities.

45

In conclusion, the freedom to pray is a fundamental human right that is essential for the practice of religion and the promotion of tolerance and understanding among different religious groups. Jews, Christians, Muslims, Druze, and Bahá'í all enjoy this freedom in many parts of the world, thanks to the protection of religious freedom in international law and the recognition of the importance of diversity and tolerance in society. It is crucial that this freedom continues to be upheld and respected in order to ensure a peaceful and harmonious coexistence among all religious communities.

"Israel its not equal rights state"arabs don't have the right to elect or to be elected"

Israel is often hailed as the only democracy in the Middle East, a beacon of freedom and equality in a region plagued by authoritarian regimes and human rights abuses. One of the key aspects that sets Israel apart as a democracy is its treatment of its Arab citizens. Arabs in Israel have the right to vote, run for office, form political parties, and participate in the democratic process just like any other citizen.

Arab citizens of Israel make up about 20% of the population, and they have representation in the Knesset, Israel's parliament. There are Arab members of the Knesset who have been elected by their

constituents and who actively participate in the political life of the country. These Arab lawmakers have not shied away from criticizing
56
the policies of the Israeli government, including its treatment of Palestinians and its security measures in the occupied territories.

Despite the challenges and discrimination that Arab citizens of Israel may face, the fact remains that they have the same rights and opportunities as their Jewish counterparts. Arab citizens can attend the same schools, work in the same professions, and live in the same neighborhoods as Jewish Israelis. While there are certainly issues of inequality and discrimination that need to be addressed, the fact that Arab citizens have a voice and a vote in the democratic process is a testament to Israel's commitment to equality and pluralism.

It is important to note that Israel is not without its flaws, and there are certainly areas where the country falls short of its democratic ideals. The ongoing conflict with the Palestinians, the treatment of Arab citizens in certain areas, and the influence of religious and nationalist elements in Israeli politics are all issues that need to be addressed. However, the fact that Arab citizens of Israel have the right to participate in the democratic process and to criticize the government is a sign of a functioning democracy.

In conclusion, Israel can be considered a real democracy in the sense that all citizens, regardless of their ethnicity or religion, have the right to participate in the political process. Arab citizens of Israel have the same rights and opportunities as Jewish citizens, and they have the ability to voice their opinions and advocate for change. While there are certainly challenges and areas for improvement, the fact that Arab citizens can vote, run for office, and form political parties is a testament to Israel's commitment to democracy and equality.

"Jews have been persecuting and murdering arabs from the begging of the

zionist movement "

Throughout history, Arabs have been involved in persecuting, raping, and murdering Jews worldwide. This can be seen in the numerous pogroms that have taken place in countries such as Iraq, Yemen, Egypt, Syria, Lebanon, and Jordan. These acts of violence have been fueled by religious, political, and social tensions that have existed between Arabs and Jews for centuries.

One of the most well-known instances of Arab persecution of Jews occurred in Iraq during the Farhud pogrom of 1941. This violent event saw the massacre of hundreds of Jews in Baghdad, as well as the looting and destruction of Jewish homes and businesses. The Farhud was a result of anti-Jewish sentiment that had been brewing in Iraq for years, fueled by Nazi propaganda and the rise of Arab nationalism.

Similarly, in Yemen, Jews have faced persecution and violence at the hands of their Arab neighbors. The Jewish community in Yemen has a long history of being marginalized and discriminated against, with

59

instances of rape, murder, and forced conversion being all too common. The situation for Yemeni Jews only worsened with the rise of Islamic extremism in the region, leading to further violence and persecution.

In Egypt, Syria, Lebanon, and Jordan, Jews have also faced persecution and violence at the hands of Arabs. Pogroms, riots, and attacks on Jewish communities have been a recurring theme in these countries, with Jews being targeted for their religion, ethnicity, and perceived political allegiances. The Arab-Israeli conflict has only served to exacerbate tensions between Arabs and Jews in these countries, leading to further violence and bloodshed.

It is important to acknowledge and condemn the history of Arab persecution of Jews worldwide. These acts of violence and discrimination have had a lasting impact on Jewish communities, leading to displacement, trauma, and loss of life. By understanding the root causes of this persecution and working towards reconciliation and peace, we can strive to create a more just and inclusive society for all.

"Jews live in peace today with Muslim and arabs"

The relationship between Jews and Arabs, particularly in the context of the Israeli-Palestinian conflict, has been marked by tension and conflict for decades. Jews often do not feel secure or at peace with Arab communities, both within Israel and worldwide. This lack of security and peace is exacerbated by the actions of some pro Palestinian demonstrators who target and attack Jewish synagogues, kosher shops, restaurants, and organizations.

One of the main reasons for the lack of peace and security felt by Jews in relation to Arab communities is the long-standing conflict between Israel and Palestine. The Israeli-Palestinian conflict is a complex and deeply rooted issue that has led to violence, bloodshed,

60

and animosity between the two sides. This conflict has spilled over into other parts of the world, leading to tensions between Jewish and Arab communities in various countries.

Pro-Palestinian demonstrations often serve as a platform for expressing anti-Israel sentiments, which can sometimes escalate into anti-Semitic attacks on Jewish establishments. These attacks are not only physical but also psychological, as they create a sense of fear and insecurity among Jewish communities. The targeting of Jewish synagogues, kosher shops, and restaurants is a clear indication of the deep-seated animosity towards Jews that exists within some pro Palestinian groups.

Furthermore, the rise of anti-Semitism within certain Muslim communities has also contributed to the lack of peace and security felt by Jews worldwide. Anti-Semitic rhetoric and actions have become increasingly prevalent in some Muslim-majority countries, leading to a sense of vulnerability among Jewish populations. This has further strained the already fragile relationship between Jews and Arabs, making it difficult for them to coexist peacefully.

In order to address the lack of peace and security felt by Jews in relation to Arab communities, it is essential to promote dialogue, understanding, and mutual respect between the two sides. Education and awareness-raising initiatives can help combat anti-Semitism and promote tolerance and acceptance of diversity. Additionally, governments and law enforcement agencies must take swift action to address and prevent anti-Semitic attacks, ensuring the safety and security of Jewish communities.

In conclusion, the lack of peace and security felt by Jews in relation to Arab communities is a complex issue that stems from the Israeli Palestinian conflict, anti-Semitic sentiments within certain Muslim communities, and the actions of some pro-Palestinian demonstrators. It is crucial to address these underlying issues and promote dialogue

61

and understanding in order to foster peaceful coexistence between Jews and Arabs. Only through mutual respect and tolerance can we create a world where all communities can live in peace and security.

"Anti israeli movements and demonstrations are not antisemitic "

Anti-Israeli movements and demonstrations are often accused of being anti-Semitic, and in many cases, this accusation holds true. While many of them harbor anti-Semitic beliefs, it is important to remark that there is no real difference between criticism of the Israeli state and discrimination against Jewish people

One of the most prominent anti-Israel movements is the Boycott, Divestment, and Sanctions (BDS) campaign, which seeks to pressure Israel to end its "occupation of Palestinian territories." Critics of BDS argue that the movement is inherently anti-Semitic because it specifically targets Israel. However, it is crucial to recognize that criticism of Israeli policies is finally 6 to anti-Semitism. The BDS movement is inherently anti-Semitic, as its primary goal is to undermine the Jewish state

That being said, there are many instances where anti-Israel activism crosses the line into anti-Semitism. Some pro-Palestinian activists may espouse hateful rhetoric or engage in discriminatory behavior towards Jewish individuals. This type of behavior is unacceptable and should be condemned. It is essential to differentiate between legitimate criticism of Israeli policies and actions that perpetuate anti Semitic stereotypes and discrimination.

In conclusion, while it is fair to label all anti-Israel movements and demonstrations as anti-Semitic, it is important to acknowledge that there are individuals within these movements who hold anti-Semitic beliefs. It is crucial to address and confront instances of anti Semitism within these movements

62

United Nations advocacy for human rights , UNRWA and others instrument"s

for helping the Palestinians refugees "

The United Nations Relief and Works Agency for Palestine Refugees in the Near East (UNRWA) has been embroiled in controversy over its alleged involvement in acts of real antisemitism, particularly in the

63

case of the October 7 massacre. This incident, which took place in 1985, saw the murder of three Israeli civilians by Palestinian terrorists in Cyprus. UNRWA has been accused of providing support to the perpetrators of this heinous act, raising serious questions about its role in perpetuating antisemitism.

The October 7 massacre was a brutal and senseless act of violence that shocked the world. Three Israeli civilians, including a mother and her two young children, were killed by Palestinian terrorists who had hijacked an Italian cruise ship. The terrorists demanded the release of Palestinian prisoners held in Israeli jails, and when their demands were not met, they carried out the cold-blooded murders.

UNRWA's involvement in this tragic event has been the subject of much scrutiny and criticism. It has been alleged that the agency provided support to the terrorists, including financial assistance and logistical help. This has raised serious concerns about UNRWA's impartiality and neutrality, as well as its commitment to upholding human rights and combating antisemitism.

Furthermore, UNRWA's involvement in the hostages taken during the October 7 massacre has also come under scrutiny. The agency has been accused of failing to protect the hostages and of not taking adequate measures to ensure their safety. This has raised questions about UNRWA's ability to fulfill its mandate of providing assistance and protection to Palestinian refugees in the region.

The allegations of UNRWA's involvement in acts of real antisemitism are deeply troubling and must be thoroughly investigated.

There are many issues that probe that horrible engagement. The agency must

be held accountable for any wrongdoing and must take immediate steps to address these serious concerns. It is imperative that UNRWA upholds the principles of impartiality, neutrality, and respect for human rights in all its operations, and that it takes concrete actions to combat antisemitism in all its forms.

64

In conclusion, the case of UNRWA's involvement in the October 7 massacre raises serious questions about the agency's commitment to combating antisemitism and upholding human rights. It is essential that UNRWA be held accountable for any wrongdoing and that it takes immediate steps to address these concerns. The agency must finish its operations and a new agency with a strong commitment to impartiality, neutrality, and respect for human rights in all its operations, and it must take concrete actions to combat antisemitism and ensure the safety and well-being of all those under its

"Jews stole land from arabs"

The accusation that Israeli colonists have been stealing Palestinian lands is a false and misleading claim. The truth is that there have been Jews who have been purchasing land from Arabs even before the establishment of the State of Israel. Prominent figures such as Baron Hirsh, Rothschild, and others have bought large extensions of land for agricultural purposes, and many Jewish settlers have arrived to cultivate these fields.

It is important to note that the acquisition of land by Jews in the region has been done through legal and legitimate means. The purchases were made through negotiations and agreements with the Arab landowners, and the transactions were conducted in accordance with the laws and regulations in place at the time. There was no theft or illegal seizure of land involved in these transactions.

65

Furthermore, the Jewish settlers who arrived in the region did so with the intention of building a home for themselves and establishing a community. They worked hard to cultivate the land and make it productive, contributing to the development and prosperity of the region. These settlers were not colonialists seeking to exploit or oppress the local population, but rather individuals seeking to build a better life for themselves and their families.

It is also worth mentioning that the Jewish presence in the region dates back thousands of years, long before the establishment of the State of Israel. Jews have a deep historical and cultural connection to the land, and their presence in the region is not a recent phenomenon. The Jewish people have a legitimate claim to the land based on historical, religious, and cultural ties.

In conclusion, the accusation that Israeli colonists have been stealing Palestinian lands is unfounded and misleading. The truth is that Jews have been purchasing land from Arabs through legal and legitimate means, and their presence in the region is based on historical and cultural ties to the land. It is important to understand the complexities of the situation and to avoid making simplistic and inaccurate accusations.

Jews and Arabs worked together thecl land of Palestine

Jews have a long history of working the land in Palestine, transforming it into productive and fertile land. However, for many years, the land in Palestine was abandoned and neglected, with no one interested in developing it. This lack of interest in land

66

development had a significant impact on the region, leading to a decline in agricultural productivity and economic growth.

One organization that played a crucial role in the development of the land in Palestine is Keren Kayemet LeIsrael (KKL), also known as the Jewish National Fund. Founded in 1901, KKL was established with the

goal of purchasing land in Palestine and developing it for Jewish settlement. The organization played a key role in transforming barren and neglected land into fertile and productive agricultural land.

KKL implemented various projects to reclaim and develop the land, including afforestation, water conservation, and soil improvement. Through these efforts, KKL was able to turn vast stretches of arid land into lush forests, fertile farmland, and thriving communities. The organization's work not only benefited the Jewish settlers but also had a positive impact on the Arab population living in the region.

Jews worked together to cultivate the land, sharing knowledge and expertise to improve agricultural practices and increase productivity, they were able to cooperate and collaborate in the development of the land, recognizing the benefits of a thriving agricultural sector, im both Moshavim and Kibutzim

However, the neglect of the land in Palestine for many years had a lasting impact on the region. The lack of investment in land development led to soil degradation, water scarcity, and a decline in agricultural output. This, in turn, had negative consequences for the economy, as agriculture was a significant source of income and employment for the local population.

Jews have a shared history of working the land in Palestine and transforming it into a productive and fertile landscape. Organizations like KKL played a crucial role in reclaiming and developing the land, turning barren stretches into thriving

67

agricultural communities. Despite the challenges and conflicts that have plagued the region, the cooperation between Jews in land development serves as a testament to the potential for collaboration and mutual benefit in the pursuit of sustainable development.

"Jews bringed the malaria to Palestine"

Throughout history, Jews have been the target of numerous accusations and stereotypes, often based on ignorance and prejudice. One particularly rare and absurd accusation was the claim that Jews brought malaria to Palestine. This accusation is not only false but also demonstrates the lengths to which anti-Semitic rhetoric can go.

Malaria has been a significant challenge for the people of Palestine and for anyone who lived or traveled to the region. The disease is transmitted through the bite of infected mosquitoes and has been a major health concern in many parts of the world, including Palestine. Jews, like all other inhabitants of the region, were not immune to the effects of malaria. Many fell ill, some became blind, and tragically, some even died from the disease.

To suggest that Jews were responsible for bringing malaria to Palestine is not only baseless but also illogical. Malaria is a disease that has been present in the region for centuries, long before the establishment of the State of Israel. TheAny scientific evidence does not support the accusation that Jews somehow introduced the disease to the regions is simply a manifestation of anti-Semitic sentiment.

68

Accusations like these are not only harmful but also dangerous. They perpetuate harmful stereotypes and fuel hatred and discrimination against Jewish people. It is important to challenge and debunk such baseless accusations and to educate others about the true causes of diseases like malaria.

In conclusion, the accusation that Jews brought malaria to Palestine is not only false but also a rare and absurd claim. Malaria has been a longstanding challenge for the people of the region, and Jews, like all others, have been affected by the disease. It is crucial to reject and challenge such baseless accusations and to promote understanding and tolerance among all people, regardless of their background or beliefs.

"Jews stole the Palestinians Organs"

The accusation that Jews have been stealing organs from Palestinians is not only absurd but also deeply offensive. This conspiracy theory has been circulating for years, perpetuating harmful stereotypes and fueling anti-Semitic sentiments. The idea that Jews would engage in such heinous and unethical practices is not

69

only baseless but also goes against the values and principles of Judaism.

It is important to note that there is no credible evidence to support these claims. The accusations are often based on hearsay and misinformation, and have been debunked by numerous reputable sources. In fact, the World Health Organization has stated that there is no evidence to suggest that organ trafficking is taking place in Israel or the Palestinian territories.

Furthermore, it is worth mentioning that many victims of Palestinian terror attacks have actually donated their organs to Palestinians and Israeli Arabs. Organ donation is a selfless act of kindness and generosity, and it is deeply troubling that such acts of compassion are being overshadowed by baseless accusations and conspiracy theories.

It is crucial to challenge and debunk these harmful myths and stereotypes. By spreading misinformation and promoting conspiracy theories, we are only perpetuating hatred and division. It is important to approach these issues with a critical and discerning eye, and to rely on credible sources and evidence.

In conclusion, the accusation that Jews have been stealing organs from Palestinians is not only absurd but also deeply offensive. It is crucial to challenge and debunk these harmful myths and stereotypes, and to promote understanding and compassion. Organ donation is a noble and selfless act, and it is important to recognize and celebrate the generosity of those who choose to donate their organs to save lives.

The UN fairly condemns Israel

The -United Nations has long been criticized for its bias against Israel, with many arguing that the organization unfairly targets and

70

condemns the country more than any other. This bias was particularly evident last year, when the United Nations condemned Israel more than all other countries combined. This level of condemnation is not only absurd, but it also highlights the unfair treatment that Israel receives from the international community.

One of the main reasons for the bias against Israel is the disproportionate focus on the Israeli-Palestinian conflict. While there are numerous conflicts and human rights abuses happening around the world, the United Nations seems to single out Israel for criticism. This focus on Israel not only ignores other important issues, but it also perpetuates a one-sided narrative that demonizes Israel and ignores the complexities of the conflict.

Furthermore, the United Nations has a history of passing resolutions that are blatantly biased against Israel. These resolutions often ignore the actions of terrorist groups like Hamas, which routinely target Israeli civilians with rockets and other acts of violence. Instead, the United Nations chooses to focus solely on Israeli actions, painting the country as the aggressor in the conflict.

In addition to the bias against Israel in the United Nations, other organizations like UNESCO, the Human Rights Council, and the Women's Organization have also been criticized for their unfair treatment of Israel. These organizations often single out Israel for condemnation, while turning a blind eye to the actions of other countries with far worse human rights records.

Overall, the bias against Israel in international organizations is not only unfair, but it is also counterproductive. By singling out Israel for condemnation, these organizations are not only perpetuating a one sided narrative, but they are also hindering the prospects for peace in the region. Instead of focusing solely on Israel, the United Nations and other international organizations should work towards a more

71

balanced and constructive approach to resolving the Israeli Palestinian conflict.

In conclusion, the bias against Israel in international organizations is a shameful and destructive phenomenon. The disproportionate focus on Israel, the biased resolutions, and the unfair treatment of the country all contribute to a toxic environment that hinders the prospects for peace in the region. It is time for the United Nations and other international organizations to reassess their approach to Israel and work towards a more fair and constructive dialogue.

"Arabs were first in Palestine and Jesus was Palestinian "

76

It is a common misconception that Arabs were the first inhabitants of Palestine and that Jesus was Palestinian. However, historical and archaeological evidence suggests otherwise. The land of Palestine has a long and complex history, with various peoples and cultures inhabiting the region over the centuries.

One of the earliest known inhabitants of Palestine were the Canaanites, who settled in the area around 3000 BC. The Canaanites were followed by the Israelites, who established the Kingdom of Israel in the region around 1000 BC. The Israelites were a Semitic people, closely related to the Arabs, but they were a distinct ethnic and cultural group with their own language, religion, and customs.

Jesus, who is a central figure in Christianity, was born and raised in the region of Judea, which is part of modern-day Israel. Jesus was a Jew, belonging to the Jewish people who had been living in the land of Israel for centuries. He practiced the Jewish faith, observed Jewish customs, and spoke the Hebrew language. There is no historical evidence to suggest that Jesus was Palestinian or that he identified as such.

The idea that Arabs were the first inhabitants of Palestine and that Jesus was Palestinian is often used to promote a particular political agenda. It is important to separate historical fact from political rhetoric and to acknowledge the complex and diverse history of the region. The land of Palestine has been home to many different peoples and cultures over the centuries, including Jews, Arabs, Christians, and Muslims.

In conclusion, it is not true that Arabs were the first in Palestine and that Jesus was Palestinian. The historical and archaeological evidence points to a much more nuanced and complex history of the region. Jesus was a Jew who lived and died in the land of Israel, and the Jewish people have a long and deep connection to the land of Palestine. It is important to understand and respect the diverse history of the region and to avoid simplifying or distorting it for political purposes.

"Arabs are the legitimate exclusive Heritage of Abraham Itzjak and Jacob "

Abraham, Itzhak, and Jacob are revered figures in both Islam and Judaism, but the claim that Islam was the first religion and that Jews took their beliefs from the Quran is simply false. Both religions have distinct histories, beliefs, and practices that have evolved over centuries.

Islam traces its origins back to the Prophet Muhammad in the 7th century CE, who received revelations from Allah that were compiled into the Quran. The religion spread rapidly throughout the Arabian Peninsula and beyond, establishing a new monotheistic faith that emphasized submission to the will of Allah. Abraham, known as Ibrahim in Islam, is considered a prophet in Islam and is revered for his unwavering faith and devotion to Allah.

Judaism, on the other hand, is one of the oldest monotheistic religions in the world, dating back to the time of Abraham, Itzhak, and Jacob in the ancient Near East. The Jewish people trace their lineage back to the patriarchs and matriarchs of the faith, who are considered the founders of the Jewish nation. The Torah, the sacred text of Judaism, contains the stories and teachings of these figures and their descendants, outlining the covenant between the Jewish people and God.

77

While there are similarities between Islam and Judaism, such as the belief in one God and the importance of ethical behavior, the two religions have distinct theological differences that have shaped their respective traditions. Islam places a strong emphasis on the teachings of the Prophet Muhammad and the Quran, while Judaism focuses on the laws and commandments found in the Torah and other sacred texts.

The claim that Jews took their beliefs from the Quran is not supported by historical evidence or religious scholarship. Judaism predates Islam by thousands of years and has its own rich tradition and heritage that have been passed down through generations. While there may be shared themes and figures between the two religions, they are distinct faiths with unique beliefs and practices.

In conclusion, Abraham, Itzhak, and Jacob are important figures in both Islam and Judaism, but the claim that Islam was the first religion and that Jews took their beliefs from the Quran is inaccurate. Both religions have deep roots in history and have developed their own distinct traditions and teachings over time. It is important to recognize and respect the unique contributions of each faith to the world's religious and cultural heritage.

"Jerusalem is the holiest city for muslims and muslims pray in direction to Jerusalem five times a day "

Even though Jerusalem holds a special place in the hearts of Muslims around the world, it is not considered the holiest city for Muslims.

The significance of Jerusalem for Muslims can be traced back to the time of Prophet Muhammad, who is believed to have ascended to heaven from the Al-Aqsa Mosque in Jerusalem during the Night Journey. This event, known as Isra and Mi'raj, is commemorated by Muslims every year during the month of Rajab.

In addition to the Night Journey, Jerusalem is also home to the Dome of the Rock, one of the most iconic landmarks in Islam. The Dome of the Rock is believed to be where Prophet Muhammad tied his winged steed, Buraq, before ascending to heaven.

Furthermore, Jerusalem is also home to the Al-Aqsa Mosque, which It is believed that Prophet Muhammad led prayers at the Al-Aqsa Mosque during his Night Journey.

However, despite the historical and spiritual significance of Jerusalem for Muslims, it is not the most important city for them. Muslims pray five times a day in the direction of Mecca, not Jerusalem. Mecca, the birthplace of Prophet Muhammad and the holiest city in Islam, holds a higher status in the eyes of Muslims compared to

Jerusalem.

In conclusion, Jerusalem is not the most important city for Islam .

Mecca remains the holiest city in Islam, and Muslims around the world direct their prayers towards it, emphasizing its importance in Islamic faith and practice.

Jerusalem, the capital of Israel, holds a central place in Jewish life and history. For thousands of years, this ancient city has been a symbol of Jewish identity, faith, and resilience. From the time of King David, who established Jerusalem as the capital of Judea, to the present day, Jerusalem has been a focal point for Jewish worship, culture, and community.

One of the most significant aspects of Jerusalem's importance to the Jewish people is its role as a place of prayer. Jews around the world face Jerusalem when they pray, as a way of connecting with the city that holds such deep spiritual significance. The Western Wall, also known as the Wailing Wall, is a sacred site where Jews come to pray and leave written prayers in the cracks of the ancient stones. This connection to Jerusalem through prayer is a powerful reminder of the enduring bond between the Jewish people and their ancestral homeland.

In addition to its religious significance, Jerusalem is also a symbol of Jewish history and heritage. The city is home to many important historical sites, including the Temple Mount, where the ancient Jewish temples once stood, and the City of David, where King David established his kingdom. These sites serve as reminders of the rich and complex history of the Jewish people, and the struggles and triumphs they have experienced over the centuries.

Today, Jerusalem continues to be a vibrant center of Jewish life, culture, and community. The city is home to a diverse population of Jews from around the world, who come to Jerusalem to study, pray, and connect with their heritage. The Old City of Jerusalem, with its narrow streets, ancient buildings, and bustling markets, is a living testament to the enduring presence of Jewish life in the city.

In conclusion, Jerusalem is a central and essential part of Jewish life. Its significance as a place of prayer, history, and community cannot be overstated. For Jews around the world, Jerusalem is not just a city, but a symbol of their faith, identity, and connection to their past. As the capital of Israel, Jerusalem will continue to play a vital role in Jewish life for generations to come.

79

Gaza the biggest jail in the world

The Palestinian claims that they have been living in a big jail in Gaza are not only absurd but also misleading. The truth is that the residents of Gaza have been living a relatively comfortable life until the outbreak of conflict in October 2007. The notion that Gaza is a prison for its inhabitants is a gross oversimplification of the complex political and social realities in the region.

It is important to acknowledge that the situation in Gaza is indeed challenging, with high levels of poverty, unemployment, and limited access to basic services. However, it is crucial to understand that these challenges are a result of the ongoing conflict between Israel and Palestine, rather than a deliberate attempt to imprison the people of Gaza.

Prior to the outbreak of conflict in 2007, Gaza was a bustling and vibrant city with a thriving economy and a rich cultural heritage. The residents of Gaza enjoyed access to education, healthcare, and other essential services, and many were able to lead fulfilling and productive lives.

The narrative of Gaza as a prison is often perpetuated by political actors seeking to garner sympathy and support for their cause. While

80

It is true that the blockade imposed by Israel has had a significant impact on the lives of Gazans, it is important to recognize that this blockade is a response to security concerns and is not intended to punish or imprison the people of Gaza.

It is also worth noting that the situation in Gaza is not solely the result of Israeli actions. The internal divisions within the Palestinian leadership, as well as the influence of extremist groups, have contributed to the instability and insecurity in the region.

In conclusion, while the challenges facing the people of Gaza are real and significant, it is important to avoid simplistic and misleading narratives that paint Gaza as a prison.

United Kingdom was a big empire that never recognized the jewish right to become an independent nation in Palestine

The Balfour Declaration, issued on November 2, 1917, by the British government, expressed support for the establishment of a national home for the Jewish people in Palestine. This declaration was a significant milestone in the movement for Jewish self-determination and played a crucial role in the eventual creation of the state of Israel in 1948.

The idea of a Jewish homeland in Palestine had been gaining momentum in the late 19th and early 20th centuries, as Jewish communities around the world sought a safe haven from persecution and discrimination. The Balfour Declaration, named after British Foreign Secretary Arthur Balfour, was a formal recognition of the Jewish people's historical connection to the land of Israel and their right to establish a national home there.

The declaration was a product of various factors, including British strategic interests in the Middle East, the influence of the Zionist movement, and a desire to gain support from Jewish communities in the United States and Russia. It was also seen as a way to counter the growing influence of Arab nationalism in the region.

The Balfour Declaration was met with both support and opposition. Jewish communities around the world welcomed it as a step towards fulfilling their long-held aspirations for a homeland in Israel. However, Arab leaders and Palestinian nationalists viewed it as a betrayal of their own aspirations for self-determination and independence.

Despite the controversy surrounding the Balfour Declaration, it laid the groundwork for the establishment of the state of Israel in 1948. The declaration was incorporated into the British Mandate for Palestine, which was established by the League of Nations in 1922. This mandate provided for the establishment of a Jewish national home in Palestine and laid the foundation for the eventual creation of the state of Israel.

The right of the Jewish people to become an independent nation in Israel is rooted in their historical and religious connection to the land. For centuries, Jews have maintained a presence in the region, despite periods of exile and persecution. The establishment of Israel as a Jewish state was seen as a way to ensure the safety and security of the Jewish people and to provide a homeland where they could live freely and practice their religion without fear of discrimination or persecution.

The Balfour Declaration and the subsequent creation of the state of Israel have been a source of pride and celebration for Jewish communities around the world. The establishment of Israel as a Jewish state has provided a sense of belonging and identity for Jews who have longed for a homeland of their own.

In conclusion, the Balfour Declaration was a pivotal moment in the movement for Jewish self-determination and the establishment of the state of Israel. It recognized the historical connection of the Jewish people to the land of Israel and affirmed their right to establish a national home there. The creation of Israel as a Jewish state has provided a safe haven for Jews around the world and has fulfilled their long-held aspirations for a homeland of their own.

The United Kingdom acted according to the Balfour declaration spirit

The 1939 White Paper issued by the British Empire severely limited Jewish immigration to Palestine at a time when Jews were facing increasing persecution in Europe. This policy not only prevented thousands of Jews from finding refuge in Palestine but also contributed to the loss of countless lives during the Holocaust. The British Empire's failure to provide a safe haven for Jewish refugees fleeing Nazi persecution stands in stark contrast to the ideals expressed in the Balfour Declaration.

The Balfour Declaration, issued in 1917, expressed support for the establishment of a Jewish homeland in Palestine. This declaration was seen as a significant step towards recognizing the rights of the Jewish people to self-determination. However, the restrictive immigration policies outlined in the 1939 White Paper contradicted the spirit of the Balfour Declaration and hindered the ability of Jews to seek refuge in Palestine during a time of great need.

The British Empire's actions in Palestine during this period highlight the complexities and contradictions of colonial rule. While the Balfour Declaration may have signaled a recognition of the Jewish people's right to a homeland, the British Empire's implementation of restrictive immigration policies demonstrated a lack of commitment to upholding this right for many Jews.

The consequences of the 1939 White Paper were devastating. Thousands of Jews who were seeking refuge from persecution in Europe were turned away from Palestine, ultimately leading to their deaths in the Holocaust. The British Empire's failure to provide a safe haven for Jewish refugees fleeing Nazi persecution not only contradicted the principles of human rights and justice but also highlighted the limitations of colonial rule in addressing complex humanitarian crises.

In conclusion, while the Balfour Declaration may have recognized the Jewish people's right to establish a homeland in Palestine, the British Empire's actions in the years following the declaration tell a different story. The restrictive immigration policies outlined in the White Papers prevented thousands of Jews from finding refuge in Palestine during a time of great need. The failure of the British Empire to provide a haven for Jewish refugees fleeing Nazi persecution underscores the challenges of navigating competing interests in the pursuit of justice and human rights. The legacy of the 1939 White Paper serves as a reminder of the importance of upholding the principles of compassion and solidarity in times of crisis.

4

"Jewish terrorism" against english and Arabs

The Jewish people have a long history of fighting against oppression and persecution, and this has been particularly evident in their struggle against English colonialism and Arab terrorism. Throughout history, the Jewish people have faced numerous challenges and threats to their existence, but they have always remained resilient and determined to defend their homeland, the land of Israel.

One of the key challenges that the Jewish people have faced in their fight for independence and sovereignty is the English colonial rule in Palestine. The British Mandate of Palestine, which was established after World War I, imposed restrictions on Jewish immigration and land ownership, making it difficult for the Jewish people to establish a homeland in their ancestral land. Despite these obstacles, the Jewish community in Palestine continued to grow and thrive, and they eventually declared the establishment of the State of Israel in 1948.

In addition to the English colonial rule, the Jewish people have also had to contend with Arab terrorism and violence. Since the early 20th century, Arab nationalist movements have sought to undermine and destroy the Jewish presence in Palestine through acts of terrorism and violence. One of the most notorious figures in this regard was the Mufti of Jerusalem, Haj Amin al-Husseini, who allied himself with the Nazis during World War II and incited violence against the Jewish population in Palestine.

Despite these challenges, the Jewish people have remained steadfast in their commitment to defending their homeland and protecting themselves from Arab terrorism. The State of Israel has developed a strong military and security apparatus to combat terrorism and defend its citizens from harm. Israeli security forces have thwarted numerous terrorist attacks and have worked tirelessly to ensure the safety and security of the Israeli people.

Furthermore, the Jewish people have also faced economic challenges in their fight for independence, particularly in the form of Arab boycotts of Palestinian goods. Arab countries have sought to economically isolate Israel and undermine its legitimacy by boycotting products made in Israeli settlements in the West Bank. Despite these efforts, Israel has continued to thrive economically and has developed a strong and diverse economy that is able to withstand external pressures.

In conclusion, the Jewish people have faced numerous challenges in their fight against English colonialism and Arab terrorism, but they have remained resilient and determined in their struggle for independence and sovereignty. Through their perseverance and commitment to defending their homeland, the Jewish people have been able to overcome these challenges and establish a thriving and prosperous state in the land of Israel. The formation of the Haganah and other Jewish paramilitary organizations in Palestine in the late 19th and early 20th centuries marked a turning point in Jewish history. These groups played a crucial role in defending the Jewish community and laying the foundation for the State of Israel. While their methods may have been controversial, their commitment to self-defense and independence cannot be denied.

9

Yom haatzmaut /Nakba , "the jews expelled the Arabs from Palestine"

Yom Ha'atzmaut, or Israeli Independence Day, is a day of celebration and remembrance for the Jewish people. It marks the establishment of the State of Israel in 1948, following the acceptance of the United Nations Partition Plan for Palestine. This plan called for the creation of separate Jewish and Arab states, with Jerusalem as an international city. The Jewish leadership accepted this plan, while the Arab leadership rejected it.

10

On the other hand, Nakba, which means "catastrophe" in Arabic, is the term used by Palestinians to describe the events surrounding the establishment of the State of Israel. For Palestinians, Nakba represents the displacement and suffering of hundreds of thousands of Palestinians who were forced to flee their homes during the 1948 Arab-Israeli War.

The contrast between Yom Ha'atzmaut and Nakba highlights the divergent narratives of the Israeli and Palestinian people. While Israelis celebrate their independence and the fulfillment of their

national aspirations, Palestinians mourn the loss of their homeland and the ongoing struggle for self-determination.

One of the critical points of contention between the two narratives is the role of violence in the conflict. The Arab armies that invaded Israel in 1948 did so with the intention of destroying the newly established state and driving the Jewish population into the sea. This aggressive stance towards the Jewish people led to a series of wars and conflicts that have shaped the region to this day.

In contrast, the Jewish leadership accepted the UN partition plan and sought to establish a peaceful coexistence with their Arab neighbors. However, the rejection of this plan by the Arab states and the subsequent attacks on Israel forced the Jewish population to defend themselves and fight for their survival.

The events of 1948, as well as subsequent conflicts in 1956, 1967, and 1973, have left a deep scar on the collective memory of both Israelis and Palestinians. The ongoing violence and animosity between the two sides have made it difficult to achieve a lasting peace in the region.

From time immemorial , the conflict has taken dimensions of horror with the rise of palestinian extremist terrorist groups like Hamas, who

11

have carried out attacks against Israeli civilians and sought to undermine the peace process. The violence and suffering by the jews have only served to deepen the divide between Israelis and Palestinians and make the prospect of a peaceful resolution seem increasingly remote.

In conclusion, the contrasting narratives of Yom Ha'atzmaut and Nakba is the absolute– truth against the history tergiversación and definitely against lies .

Israel is perpetuating the Occupation

The Israeli Palestine conflict is a complex and contentious issue that has been ongoing for decades. The roots of this conflict can be traced back to biblical times, with the Jewish people claiming a historical connection to the land of Israel. Indeed, the Jews see themselves as returning home to their ancestral land, a land that holds deep profound and cultural significance for them.

The story of the Jewish people in the land of Israel dates back thousands of years, with figures such as Abraham, Isaac, and Jacob considered the patriarchs of the Jewish people. Jesus himself was a Jew, born in Bethlehem, further solidifying the connection between the Jewish people and the land of Israel. Judea and Samaria, areas that are now part of the West Bank, have long been considered part of the Jewish homeland.

The term "Palestine" itself is a name given by the Romans as a punishment to the Jewish people after a failed revolt. It was not until the 20th century that the term came to be associated with the Arab population living in the region. The conflict between Israelis and

Palestinians is deeply rooted in this historical and religious context, with both sides claiming a right to the land.

12

In recent years, tensions between Israelis and Palestinians have only escalated, with violence and conflict becoming a regular occurrence. The Israeli supposed occupation of Palestinian territories, particularly in the West Bank and Gaza Strip, has been a significant point of contention. The construction of Israeli settlements in these areas has been a source of conflict, with Palestinians viewing them as a violation of their rights and a barrier to a future Palestinian state.

The international community has been divided on the issue, with some countries supporting Israel's right to defend itself and others condemning the occupation and calling for a two-state solution. The Arab world has also been involved in the conflict, with some countries boycotting Israeli goods in solidarity with the so-called Palestinian cause.

In conclusion, the Israeli occupation of Palestine doesn't really exist , there are lands in dispute. The conflict is a complex and multifaceted issue that is deeply rooted in history, religion, and politics. Only through the compromise can a lasting peace be achieved in the region, that requires that the Palestinian Authority will stop paying a permanent pension to those who attempt to kill jews. And also it should end the hate jewish education .

"Israel is an Apartheid State"

There is a common misconception that Israel practices apartheid, a system of institutionalized racial segregation and discrimination. However, this assertion is not only inaccurate but also misleading. In reality, Israel is a diverse and inclusive society where minorities are integrated and have equal rights and opportunities.

13

One of the key reasons why Israel cannot be compared to apartheid South Africa is its legal framework. Israel is a democratic state with a legal system that guarantees equal rights and protections for all its citizens, regardless of their ethnicity or religion. The Israeli Declaration of Independence explicitly states that the country "will ensure complete equality of social and political rights to all its inhabitants irrespective of religion, race or sex." This commitment to equality is enshrined in Israel's Basic Laws, which serve as the country's constitution.

Furthermore, Israel is a multicultural society where people of different backgrounds coexist peacefully. Arab citizens of Israel, who make up about 20% of the population, have the same rights as Jewish citizens. They can vote, run for office, and serve in the military. In fact, Arab

citizens have been elected to the Knesset, Israel's parliament, and have held positions in the government and judiciary.

In addition, Israel has made significant efforts to integrate its minority communities into all aspects of society. Arab citizens have access to education, healthcare, and employment opportunities. Israeli universities and hospitals are open to all citizens, regardless of their background. Arab students attend Israeli universities, where they study alongside Jewish students. Arab doctors and nurses work in Israeli hospitals, providing care to patients of all backgrounds.

Moreover, Israel has made progress in promoting diversity and inclusion in its society. Organizations and initiatives have been established to empower minority communities and promote dialogue and understanding between different groups. For example, the Abraham Initiatives works to advance equality and shared society between Jews and Arabs in Israel. The Hand in Hand network of bilingual schools brings together Jewish and Arab students to learn and grow together.

14

In conclusion, the claim that Israel practices apartheid is unfounded and misleading. Israel is a democratic and inclusive society where minorities are integrated and have equal rights and opportunities. The country's legal framework, multiculturalism, and efforts to promote diversity and inclusion all demonstrate that Israel is not an apartheid state. It is essential to recognize and celebrate the progress that Israel has made in building a society where all citizens can live and thrive together.

Israel machinist Patriarchal state "

"Israel is a state with many Women rights abuses "

Women's rights in Israel have come a long way since the country's establishment in 1948. Israel is known for being a progressive and democratic country, and this is reflected in the rights and opportunities that women have in various aspects of society, including in universities, the state, and the army.

In universities, women in Israel have equal access to education and are encouraged to pursue higher education and professional careers. In fact, women make up the majority of students in Israeli universities, and they have the same opportunities as men to study in any field they choose. This has led to a significant increase in the number of women in leadership positions in academia, as well as in other fields such as business, politics, and the arts.

In the state, women in Israel have the right to vote and run for political office. Israel has had several female prime ministers, including Golda Meir and more recently, Tzipi Livni. Women also hold key positions in the Israeli government, such as ministers, members of parliament, and judges. The Israeli government has also implemented policies to promote gender equality, such as affirmative action programs and anti-discrimination laws.

15

In the army, women in Israel have the right to serve in the military and are encouraged to do so. Women serve in combat roles, as well as in other positions in the army, and they have the same opportunities for advancement as men. The Israeli army has also implemented policies

to prevent sexual harassment and discrimination against women, and to promote gender equality in the military.

Overall, women in Israel have made significant progress in terms of their rights and opportunities in various aspects of society. However, there are still challenges that women face, such as gender-based violence, wage disparities, and underrepresentation in certain fields. It is important for the Israeli government and society to continue to work towards achieving full gender equality and empowering women to reach their full potential.

"Israel is a Racist state"

Israel is often accused of being a racist state, particularly in its treatment of minority groups such as Arabs and Palestinians. However, this accusation is not entirely accurate. In fact, Israel is a country that grants equal rights to all its citizens, regardless of their ethnicity or religion.

16

One of the main arguments against Israel being a racist state is the fact that it is a democracy. In a true democracy, all citizens are granted equal rights and opportunities, regardless of their background. Israel is no exception to this rule. Arab citizens of Israel have the same rights as Jewish citizens, including the right to vote, freedom of speech, and access to education and healthcare. In fact, Arab citizens of Israel have even served in the Israeli government, including in the Knesset, the country's parliament.

Furthermore, Israel is a country that prides itself on its diversity. It is home to a large number of minority groups, including Arabs, Druze, Bedouins, and Circassians. These groups are free to practice their own religions and traditions, and many have achieved success in various fields, including politics, business, and the arts. In fact, Israel is one of the few countries in the Middle East where minority groups have the opportunity to thrive and succeed.

Another argument against Israel being a racist state is the fact that it has laws in place to protect minority rights. For example, Israel's Declaration of Independence guarantees equal rights for all citizens, regardless of their ethnicity or religion. The country also has anti discrimination laws that prohibit discrimination on the basis of race, religion, or nationality. While there have been instances of discrimination and prejudice in Israel, as there are in any country, the government has taken steps to address these issues and promote equality for all its citizens.

In conclusion, Israel is not a racist state. While there are certainly challenges and tensions between different ethnic and religious groups in the country, Israel is a democracy that grants equal rights to all its citizens. Minority groups in Israel have the same opportunities and protections as the majority population, and the country has laws in place to ensure that discrimination is not tolerated. Israel's commitment to diversity and equality sets it apart from many other countries in the region, and it is important essential

recognize and celebrate the progress that has been made in promoting tolerance and understanding among all its citizens.

"Zionism is racism "

Zionism, often spelled as Zionism, is a political and nationalistic movement that advocates for the establishment of a Jewish homeland in the land of Israel. Contrary to popular belief, Zionism is not inherently racist. It is essential to understand the historical context and motivations behind the movement in order to dispel any misconceptions.

The roots of Zionism can be traced back to Theodor Herzl, an Austro-Hungarian journalist who is considered the father of modern Zionism. Herzl believed that the only solution to the persecution and discrimination faced by Jews in Europe was the establishment of a Jewish state. In 1897, he convened the First Zionist Congress in Basel, Switzerland, where the foundations of the Zionist movement were laid.

The Second Zionist Congress, held in 1898, further solidified the goals and objectives of the movement. It was at this congress that the World Zionist Organization was established, with the aim of promoting Jewish settlement in Palestine and fostering Jewish national identity.

The Third Zionist Congress, held in 1899, saw the adoption of the "Basel Program," which called for the establishment of a legally

18

assured home for the Jewish people in Palestine. This program laid the groundwork for the eventual establishment of the State of Israel.

One of the key figures in the development of Zionism was Leon Pinsker, a Russian Jewish physician and writer. In his seminal work, "Auto-Emancipation," Pinsker argued that the only way for Jews to achieve true emancipation was through the establishment of a Jewish state. His ideas laid the intellectual foundation for the Zionist movement.

Chaim Weizmann, a chemist and Zionist leader, made significant contributions to the Zionist cause. He played a crucial role in securing the Balfour Declaration in 1917, which expressed the British government's support for the establishment of a Jewish national home in Palestine.

David Ben-Gurion, the first Prime Minister of Israel, was instrumental in the establishment of the State of Israel in 1948. His leadership and vision were crucial in the successful realization of the Sionist dream.

In conclusion, Zionism is not a racist ideology, but rather a nationalistic movement that seeks to secure the rights and homeland of the Jewish people. It is important to understand the historical context and motivations behind the movement in order to appreciate its significance. The establishment of the State of Israel is a testament to the perseverance and determination of the Zionist movement.

Bedouins, , Muslims, christians and druze don't enjoy full citizenship in israel

Arabs, Muslims, Druze, Chackeshim, Christians, Bedouins, and Bahais in Israel have never faced persecution and enjoy full

19

citizenship rights, thanks to the country's history of religious tolerance and respect for diversity. These groups have been able to coexist peacefully and thrive in a diverse society, contributing to the cultural, social, and economic fabric of the country.

Arabs have been an integral part of Israel for centuries, with a rich cultural heritage and strong ties to the land. They have played a significant role in shaping the country's history and have contributed to its development in various fields such as politics, business, and the arts. Arabs in Israel enjoy full citizenship rights and are represented in all levels of government, demonstrating the country's commitment to inclusivity and equality.

Muslims, who make up a significant portion of the population, also enjoy full citizenship rights and are free to practice their religion without fear of persecution. The country's long history of religious tolerance has allowed Muslims to worship freely in mosques and observe religious holidays without interference, fostering a sense of community and belonging.

Druze, a religious minority in Israel, have also been able to live peacefully and practice their faith without fear of persecution. They are recognized as a distinct religious group and have their own religious courts and institutions, allowing them to maintain their cultural identity while integrating into society. Druze have made significant contributions to Israel's cultural and social fabric, further enriching the country's diverse tapestry.

Chackeshim, Christians, Bedouins, and Baha'is are also minority groups in Israel who have never faced persecution. They enjoy full citizenship rights and are free to practice their religion and culture without fear of discrimination. Christians have a long history in Israel and have made significant contributions to its cultural and social fabric, while Bedouins have been able to maintain their traditional way of life while integrating into modern society. Bahais, a religious

20

minorities have been able to practice their faith openly and are respected for their contributions to society.

In conclusion, Arabs, Muslims, Druze, Chackeshim, Christians, Bedouins, and Bahais in Israel have never been persecuted and enjoy full citizenship rights. The country's history of religious tolerance and respect for diversity has allowed these groups to coexist harmoniously and thrive in a diverse society. Israel's commitment to inclusivity and equality has created a welcoming environment for all its citizens, regardless of their background or beliefs.

:Israel its s Colonialist state"

Israel is a country that has often been accused of being a colonialist state due to its establishment in 1948 and its ongoing conflict with the Palestinian people. However, it is essential to understand that Israel is not a colonialist state, but rather a nation that has a legitimate claim to its land and has a right to exist as a sovereign state.

One of the keys against Israel being a colonialist state is the fact that the Jewish people have a historical connection to the land of Israel.

The Jewish people have lived in the region for thousands of years and have maintained a continuous presence in the land, even during times of exile and persecution. The establishment of the modern state of Israel in 1948 was a culmination of the Jewish people's long-standing desire to return to their ancestral homeland.

Furthermore, Israel is a democratic state that guarantees equal rights to all its citizens, regardless of their religion or ethnicity. Arab citizens of Israel have the same rights as Jewish citizens, including the right to vote, freedom of speech, and access to education and healthcare. This stands in stark contrast to colonialist states, which typically discriminate against indigenous populations and deny them basic fundamentals and freedoms.

21

Additionally, Israel has made numerous efforts to reach a peaceful resolution to its conflict with the Palestinian people. Israel has repeatedly expressed its willingness to negotiate a two-state solution that would allow for the creation of a Palestinian state alongside Israel. However, the Palestinian leadership has consistently rejected these offers and has instead resorted to violence and terrorism in an attempt to achieve its goals.

In conclusion, Israel is not a colonialist state, but a nation with a legitimate claim to its land and a right to exist as a sovereign state. The Jewish people have a historical connection to the land of Israel, and Israel is a democratic state that guarantees equal rights to all its citizens. Israel has also made efforts to reach a peaceful resolution to its conflict with the Palestinian people. It is essential to recognize these facts and to support efforts to achieve a lasting peace in the region.

"Israel its an Imperialist state"

Israel is a country that has often been accused of being an imperialist state, but this accusation is not accurate. The Jewish people have a long and deep connection to the land of Israel, dating back thousands of years. This connection is not based on imperialism, but on a shared history, culture, and religion.

22

The Jewish people have a strong historical tie to the land of Israel, which is often referred to as the "Promised Land" in the Bible. According to Jewish tradition, the land of Israel was promised to the Jewish people by God, and it has always been seen as their ancestral homeland. Throughout history, Jews have faced persecution and exile, but their connection to the land of Israel has remained strong.

In the late 19th and early 20th centuries, the Zionist movement emerged, calling for the establishment of a Jewish state in the land of Israel. This movement was not driven by imperialist ambitions, but by a desire to create a safe haven for the Jewish people, who had faced centuries of discrimination and violence in other countries. The establishment of the state of Israel in 1948 was a fulfillment of this dream, and it was seen as a homecoming for the Jewish people.

The accusation of Israel being an imperialist state is often based on the conflict with the Palestinian people, who also have historical ties to the land of Israel. However, it is imporessentialecognize that the Jewish people have a legitimate claim to the land as well. The Jewish people have lived in the land of Israel for thousands of years, and their connection to the land is not based on conquest or colonization, but on a shared history and culture.

In 2016, UNESCO passed Resolution 2335, which denied the Jewish connection to the land of Israel and referred to the Western Wall in Jerusalem as a Muslim holy site. This decision was widely criticized by Israel and its supporters, who saw it as an attempt to erase Jewish history and heritage. The resolution was seen as a denial of the Jewish people's legitimate claim to the land of Israel, and it sparked outrage among Jewish communities around the world.

23

In conclusion, Israel is not an imperialist state, but a country with a strong and legitimate connection to the land of Israel. The Jewish people have a long history in the land, and their claim to it is based on their shared history, culture, and religion. The accusation of imperialism is unfounded and ignores the deep ties that the Jewish people have to the land of Israel. It is important to recognize and respect the Jewish connection to the land, and to work towards a peaceful resolution to the conflict with the Palestinian people that respects the rights and histories of both communities.

The false accusation : Israel's human rights abuse?" , indeed Israeli army is the worldwide one

The Israeli army, also known as the Israel Defense Forces (IDF), has often been the subject of false accusations regarding human rights abuses. However, upon closer examination, it becomes clear that the IDF is actually one of the most ethical armies in the world.

One of the key reasons why the IDF is considered to be ethical is the fact that its officials lead by example. The IDF places a strong emphasis on moral values and ethical behavior, and this is reflected in the actions of its leaders. IDF officials are held to a high standard of conduct, and they are expected to uphold the principles of justice, integrity, and respect for human rights. This commitment to ethical leadership sets the tone for the entire organization and ensures that moral behavior is prioritized at all levels of the IDF.

Furthermore, the IDF is dedicated to protecting civilian lives, even at great significance to its own soldiers. The IDF goes to great lengths to minimize civilian casualties in conflict zones, often putting its own soldiers in harm's way in order to protect innocent civilians. This commitment to the protection of civilians is a testament to the ethical values that guide the IDF's actions.

24

In addition, the IDF operates under a strict code of conduct that governs the behavior of its soldiers. This code of conduct emphasizes the importance of respecting human rights, upholding the rule of law, and treating all individuals with dignity and respect. Soldiers who violate this code of conduct are held accountable for their actions, further demonstrating the IDF's commitment to ethical behavior.

Overall, the IDF's track record of ethical conduct and commitment to protecting civilian lives sets it apart as one of the most ethical armies in the world. Despite false accusations of human rights abuses, the IDF remains dedicated to upholding the highest standards of ethical behavior and ensuring the safety and well-being of all individuals in conflict zones.

"Israel committed genocide "

Israel has long been a controversial topic in international politics, with accusations of genocide and human rights violations being leveled against the Jewish state. However, it is essential to note that Israel has never committed genocide, and in fact, many Israeli soldiers have been murdered in the line of duty while trying to protect Palestinian civilians.

The Israeli military, known as the Israel Defense Forces (IDF), has always taken great care to minimize civilian casualties in its

25

operations. This commitment to protecting innocent lives dates back to the pre-state militias that eventually formed the IDF. These militias, such as the Haganah and the Palmach, were instrumental in the establishment of the State of Israel in 1948 and laid the foundation for the IDF's ethos of moral conduct in warfare.

Throughout its history, the IDF has faced numerous challenges in trying to protect both Israeli citizens and Palestinian civilians. In the ongoing conflict with Palestinian militant groups, such as Hamas and Islamic Jihad, Israeli soldiers have often found themselves in dangerous situations where they must make split second decisions to protect themselves and others. Tragically, many Israeli soldiers have paid the ultimate price for their dedication to their country and their commitment to upholding moral standards in the midst of conflict.

One of the most painful aspects of this reality is the fact that the bodies of these fallen soldiers are sometimes used as bargaining chips by Palestinian militants. In some cases, the bodies of slain Israeli soldiers have been withheld by militant groups in an attempt to extract concessions from the Israeli government. This cruel tactic adds an extra layer of grief and suffering to the families of these soldiers, who must endure the uncertainty of not knowing the fate of their loved ones.

Despite these challenges, the IDF continues to uphold its commitment to protecting innocent lives and maintaining the highest ethical standards in its operations. Israeli soldiers undergo rigorous training in international humanitarian law and are held accountable for their actions through a system of military justice. The IDF also conducts thorough investigations into any allegations of misconduct or violations of human rights, demonstrating its commitment to transparency and accountability.

In conclusion, Israel has never committed genocide, and the sacrifices made by Israeli soldiers in the defense of their country and

26

the protection of Palestinian civilians should not be overlooked. The IDF's commitment to moral conduct in warfare and its efforts to minimize civilian casualties are a testament to the values of the Jewish state and its dedication to upholding human rights. The bodies of fallen soldiers should never be used as political bargaining chips, and all parties involved in the conflict should strive to find peaceful solutions that respect the dignity and humanity of all individuals involved.

The real intentions of arabs in the Wars was to sent the jews to the sea

The Arab-Israeli conflict has been a long-standing and complex issue that has spanned several decades. Throughout the various wars that have taken place between Arab nations and Israel, there has been a prevailing belief that the real intentions of the Arabs were to "send the Jews to the sea." This phrase has been used to suggest that the ultimate goal of the Arab nations was to eradicate the Jewish population in Israel and push them into the Mediterranean Sea.

The first major conflict between Arab nations and Israel took place in 1947-1949, known as the Arab-Israeli War. During this time, several Arab nations, including Egypt, Jordan, Syria, and Iraq, launched attacks on the newly established state of Israel. The Arab nations were motivated by a desire to prevent the creation of a Jewish state in the region and to reclaim land that they believed rightfully belonged to the Palestinians. However, the outcome of the war resulted in Israel gaining control of more territory than it had been allocated by the United Nations partition plan.

In the years following the Arab-Israeli War, tensions between Arab nations and Israel continued to escalate. The Suez Crisis of 1956 saw Israel, along with Britain and France, launch a military campaign against Egypt in response to the nationalization of the Suez Canal. The Arab nations viewed this as an act of aggression and a threat to their sovereignty, leading to further hostilities between the two sides.

27

The Six-Day War of 1967 was a turning point in the Arab-Israeli conflict, as Israel launched a preemptive strike against Egypt, Jordan, and Syria, resulting in a decisive victory for Israel. The war saw Israel gain control of the Sinai Peninsula, the West Bank, the Golan Heights, and East Jerusalem. The Arab nations were left reeling from the defeat, leading to further animosity and resentment towards Israel.

The Yom Kippur War of 1973 saw Egypt and Syria launch a surprise attack on Israel during the Jewish holiday of Yom Kippur. The Arab nations sought to regain territory lost in the Six-Day War and to assert their dominance in the region. The war resulted in heavy casualties on both sides but ultimately ended in a ceasefire, with Israel maintaining control of the territories it had captured.

In recent years, the Arab-Israeli conflict has continued to simmer, with sporadic outbreaks of violence and tensions between the two sides. The phrase "send the Jews to the sea" has been used to encapsulate the deep-seated animosity and hostility that exists between Arab nations and Israel. While the Arab nations have denied any intention of eradicating the Jewish population in Israel, the phrase serves as a reminder of the underlying tensions and grievances that have fueled the conflict for decades of anti zionist and open antisemitism.

In conclusion, the real intentions of the Arabs in the various wars with Israel have been to eliminate the jewish presence in the land of Israel While the phrase "send the Jews to the sea" may be seen as a simplification of the Arab nations' motivations, it does highlight the deep-seated animosity and hostility that have characterized the Arab regarding Jews presence in the middle east and especially in the country of Israel The ongoing struggle for land, resources, and nationalism is base in the old antisemitism

28

29

UNRWA and the real role of the UN

The United Nations Relief and Works Agency for Palestine Refugees in the Near East (UNRWA) is an organization that was established in 1949 to provide assistance and support to Palestinian refugees in the Middle East. However, in recent years, there have been allegations that UNRWA has been openly supporting the terrorist organization Hamas, which has raised questions about the real role of the United Nations in the region.

One of the most concerning allegations against UNRWA is that some of its workers have participated in attacks against Israelis. For example, on October 7th, there was a massacre of Israelis in which UNRWA workers were allegedly involved. This raises serious questions about the neutrality and impartiality of UNRWA and whether the organization is truly dedicated to providing humanitarian assistance to those in need. Those accusations have been proved and sadly many "humanitarian workers" slaughtered jewish babies and participated in the mass violations against jewish girls and woman

The role of the United Nations is to promote peace, security, and human rights around the world. However, if UNRWA is indeed supporting terrorist organizations like Hamas, it undermines the credibility and effectiveness of the United Nations as a whole. It is essential that the United Nations remains impartial and does not take sides in conflicts, as this is crucial for maintaining peace and stability in the region.

It is important to remark on the massive failure of the United Nations to investigate these allegations and take appropriate actions . UNRWA indeed had been supporting terrorist organizations. The United Nations must uphold its principles of neutrality and impartiality and ensure that its agencies are not involved in activities that undermine peace and security in the region.

30

In conclusion, the allegations against UNRWA for supporting Hamas and participating in attacks against Israelis are deeply concerning and raise serious questions about the real fundamentals of the United Nations in the Middle East. It is essential for the United Nations to investigate these allegations thoroughly and take appropriate action to ensure that its agencies are upholding the principles of neutrality and impartiality. Only then can the United Nations truly fulfill its mission of promoting peace, security, and human rights around the world.

Palestinian refugees and there is no Jewish refugees
32

The issue of Palestinian refugees and Jewish refugees is a complex and deeply rooted one, with historical and political implications that have shaped the Middle East for decades. The origins of the Palestinian refugee crisis can be traced back to the Arab-Israeli conflict, which began in the late 1940s with the establishment of the state of Israel.

As tensions between Arab states and Israel escalated, hundreds of thousands of Palestinians were forced to flee their homes and seek refuge in neighboring countries.

The plight of Palestinian refugees is a tragic and ongoing humanitarian crisis, with millions of Palestinians still living in refugee camps in the West Bank, Gaza Strip, Lebanon, Jordan, and Syria. These refugees face a myriad of challenges, including limited access to essential basic services such as healthcare, education, and employment, as well as ongoing political instability and violence in the region.

On the other hand, the issue of Jewish refugees is often overlooked in discussions of the Middle East conflict. Throughout history, Jews have faced persecution and discrimination in Arab countries, leading to mass exodus from countries such as Yemen, Iraq, Syria, Egypt, and Lebanon. These Jewish refugees were forced to leave behind their homes, possessions, and communities, and many resettled in Israel or other countries.

The experiences of Palestinian and Jewish refugees highlight the complexities of the Arab-Israeli conflict and the deep-seated animosities between the two sides. Both groups have suffered displacement and loss, and both have legitimate claims to their ancestral lands. However, the political and historical context of the conflict has made it difficult to find a resolution that satisfies the needs and aspirations of both Palestinian and Jewish refugees.

In order to address the issue of Palestinian and Jewish refugees, it is essential to recognize the historical injustices and traumas that have

33

shaped their experiences. Efforts must be made to provide humanitarian assistance and support to both groups, as well as to work towards a just and lasting resolution to the Arab-Israeli conflict. This will require dialogue, compromise, and a commitment to peace and reconciliation from all parties involved.

In conclusion, the issue of Palestinian and Jewish refugees is a complex and multifaceted one that requires a nuanced understanding of the historical, political, and humanitarian dimensions of the Arab Israeli conflict. By acknowledging the experiences and rights of both groups, and working towards a just and equitable solution, we can begin to address the longstanding grievances and injustices that have plagued the region for generations.

From the river to the sea, Palestine will be free

From the river to the sea Palestine will be free. It's an antisemitic and judeophobia action . It is a dangerous slogan

The phrase "from the river to the sea, Palestine will be free" has become a common familiar among anti-Israel protesters in cities like London, New York, and Sydney. While on the surface it may seem like a call for Palestinian liberation, a closer examination reveals a much darker and more sinister meaning.

The phrase is often used by those who seek the elimination of the Jewish state of Israel and the annihilation of the Israeli population. It is a call for the destruction of Israel and the expulsion of its Jewish inhabitants. This is not a call for peace or justice, but rather a call for violence and hatred.

What is particularly troubling about this phrase is that many etowho chant it do not even know what river or sea they are referring to.

34

The phrase is vague and ambiguous, allowing for different interpretations and meanings. This lack of specificity only adds to the dangerous and inflammatory nature of the chant.

Furthermore, the phrase is deeply rooted in anti-Semitism. It seeks to deny the Jewish people their right to self-determination and their right to exist as a sovereign nation. It perpetuates harmful stereotypes and prejudices against Jews, painting them as oppressors and

aggressors.

It is important to condemn it for what it is: a call for violence, hatred, and the destruction of Israel. It is a dangerous and inflammatory slogan that has no place in any legitimate discourse on the Israeli Palestinian conflict.

In conclusion, the phrase "from the river to the sea, Palestine will be free" is not a call for peace or justice, but rather a call for the elimination of Israel and the Jewish people. It is a deeply troubling and anti-Semitic slogan that should be condemned by all those who seek a peaceful resolution to the Israeli-Palestinian conflict.

.

The Palestinian are the real victims

The media plays a crucial role in shaping public opinion and perceptions of global conflicts. However, there have been instances
35
where media outlets, such as Al Jazeera, have been accused of bias and misrepresentation in their coverage of conflicts in the Middle East, particularly when it comes to portraying Palestinians as victims.

One of the most notable examples of this bias is the frequent use of images from Iraq or the civil war in Syria to depict Palestinian victims. By using images from other conflicts to represent the Palestinian struggle, media outlets like Al Jazeera are perpetuating a false narrative that seeks to garner sympathy for the Palestinian cause. This distorts the reality of the situation on the ground and undermines the credibility of the media as a source of unbiased information.

Furthermore, there have been instances where media outlets, including the BBC, have erroneously blamed Israel for conflicts in the region. This type of misinformation not only fuels anti-Israel sentiment but also perpetuates stereotypes and prejudices against the Jewish state. It is essential for media outlets to uphold journalistic integrity and accuracy in their reporting to avoid spreading false information and inciting further conflict.

In addition to biased reporting, the Spanish press has been widely criticized for its anti-Semitic prejudices and preconceived notions. This type of discriminatory language and rhetoric only serves to perpetuate negative stereotypes and fuel hatred towards the Jewish community. It is crucial for media outlets to be mindful of the language they use and to avoid perpetuating harmful stereotypes and prejudices.

In conclusion, the media plays a significant role in shaping public perceptions of global conflicts, particularly in the Middle East. It is essential for media outlets to uphold journalistic integrity, accuracy, and impartiality in their reporting to avoid spreading misinformation and perpetuating biases. By holding media outlets accountable for

36

By reporting, we can ensure that the public is informed accurately and objectively about complex conflicts in the region.

Progressive left responsable actions in support of the Palestinians cause

Progressive left wing uneducated , ignorant and prejudice against jews And Israel

The progressive left wing has long been associated with advocating for social justice, equality, and human rights. However, there is a troubling trend within this movement of uneducated, ignorant, and prejudiced views towards Jews and Israel. This bias is rooted in a distorted and one-sided understanding of the Israeli-Palestinian conflict, which often demonizes Israel as a white colonialist imperialist entity.

It is important to recognize that Israel is not the caricature that the progressive left wing has painted it to be. Israel is a diverse and vibrant democracy that has faced numerous security threats and challenges since its establishment in 1948. The Jewish people have a

37

long and complex history, including centuries of persecution and discrimination, culminating in the horrors of the Holocaust during World War II.

The left wing is equilibrate and don't have any bias against Israel

Despite this history, the progressive left wing often portrays Israel as an oppressive and illegitimate state, while ignoring the legitimate security concerns and historical rights of the Jewish people. This bias is fueled by a lack of education and understanding of the complexities of the Israeli-Palestinian conflict, as well as a tendency to view the world through a simplistic and binary lens of oppressor versus oppressed.

This prejudice against Jews and Israel is reminiscent of the anti Semitic propaganda that was used by the Nazis to justify their persecution and extermination of the Jewish people. The infamous Nazi leader Adolf Eichmann famously said, "Lie, lie, and something will prevail." This mentality of spreading falsehoods and misinformation about Jews and Israel in order to advance a political agenda is deeply troubling and dangerous.

It is concerning that many socialist and social democratic parties worldwide have adopted this biased and prejudiced view of Israel without critically examining the facts and engaging in open and honest dialogue. This lack of critical thinking and intellectual rigor has led to a situation where anti-Semitic tropes and stereotypes are perpetuated under the guise of progressive politics.

In order to combat this prejudice and ignorance, it is essential for the progressive left wing to educate themselves about the complexities of the Israeli-Palestinian conflict, engage in respectful and informed dialogue with all parties involved, and reject the demonization and dehumanization of any group of people. It is only through a commitment to truth, justice, and empathy that we can work towards a more peaceful and just world for all.

38

Israel is not a colonialistic, fascist Imperialist state, Indeed is the opposite that the extreme left tried to establish.

Israel is a country that has often been accused of being a colonialistic, fascist imperialist state by the extreme left. However, upon closer examination, it becomes clear that these accusations are unfounded and do not accurately reflect the reality of the situation. In fact, Israel is the opposite of a colonialistic, fascist imperialist state and has a long history of fighting against such ideologies.

First and foremost, it is important to understand the history of Israel and how it came to be. Israel was established in 1948 as a homeland for the Jewish people, who had been persecuted and marginalized for centuries. The establishment of Israel was not an act of colonialism, but rather a response to the need for a safe haven for the Jewish people. In fact, Israel has a diverse population that includes Jews, Arabs, Christians, and other ethnic and religious groups, all of whom have equal rights under the law.

Furthermore, Israel has a democratic government that is based on the principles of freedom, equality, and justice. The Israeli government is elected by the people and operates under a system of checks and balances that ensures the protection of individual rights and liberties. This stands in stark contrast to fascist regimes, which are characterized by authoritarian rule and the suppression of dissent.

In addition, Israel has a strong commitment to human rights and has a vibrant civil society that actively works to promote and protect the rights of all its citizens. Israel has a free press, independent judiciary, and a robust system of civil liberties that allow for the free expression of ideas and opinions. This is not the hallmark of a fascist state, but rather a sign of a healthy and functioning democracy.

Moreover, Israel has a long history of fighting against imperialism and colonialism. Israel has been a vocal supporter of the rights of
39

oppressed peoples around the world and has consistently spoken out against the injustices of colonialism and imperialism. Israel has also been a strong advocate for peace and has made numerous efforts to reach a peaceful resolution to the conflict with the Palestinians.

In conclusion, Israel is not a colonialistic, fascist imperialist state, as some on the extreme left have claimed. Israel is a diverse, democratic country that is committed to the principles of freedom, equality, and justice. Israel has a long history of fighting against imperialism and colonialism and has worked tirelessly to promote human rights and peace. It is important to recognize the true nature of Israel and not succumb to false and misleading accusations.

Israel racism against blacks and other minorities

Israel is a melting pot of cultures and backgrounds, with people from all over the world coming together to form a diverse and vibrant society. Over the years, Israel has successfully integrated people from Russia, Iraq, Argentina, and Yemen, among other countries. This integration has been facilitated through various programs such as the Russian aliyah, the Ethiopian aliyah, and the absorption of Eritrean refugees.

The Russian aliyah, or immigration of Jews from the former Soviet Union, has been one of the largest waves of immigration to Israel. Since the collapse of the Soviet Union in the early 1990s, over one
million Russian-speaking Jews have made aliyah to Israel. These immigrants have brought with them a rich cultural heritage and have made significant contributions to Israeli society in various fields such as science, technology, and the arts.

Similarly, Jews from Iraq have also made aliyah to Israel, bringing with them their unique traditions and customs. Despite facing 40

challenges in integrating into Israeli society, many Iraqi Jews have successfully established themselves in Israel and have become active members of the community.

In addition to the Russian and Iraqi immigrants, Israel has also welcomed immigrants from Argentina and Yemen. Jews from Argentina have brought with them a vibrant Latin American culture, while Yemenite Jews have preserved their ancient traditions and customs in Israel. The integration of these diverse communities has enriched Israeli society and has contributed to the country's cultural tapestry.

One of the most significant challenges in integrating immigrants into Israeli society has been the absorption of Ethiopian Jews. The Ethiopian aliyah, which began in the 1980s, has faced numerous obstacles, including language barriers, cultural differences, and socioeconomic challenges. However, through various government programs and initiatives, many Ethiopian immigrants have successfully integrated into Israeli society and have become active members of the community.

Another group that has sought refuge in Israel is Eritrean refugees. Eritrea, a country in East Africa, has been plagued by political instability and human rights abuses, leading many Eritreans to seek asylum in Israel. Despite facing challenges in integrating into Israeli society, many Eritrean refugees have found a new home in Israel and have been able to rebuild their lives.

In conclusion, Israel's successful integration of people from Russia, Iraq, Argentina, Yemen, Ethiopia, and Eritrea is a testament to the country's commitment to diversity and inclusivity. Through various programs and initiatives, Israel has been able to welcome immigrants from around the world and provide them with the support they need to thrive in their new home. The integration of these diverse

41

communities have enriched Israeli society and have strengthened the country's cultural fabric.

42

"Arabs leaders don't enjoy free of speech"

Israel is a country of democratic values. The case of arabs anti semitic parliament members who are working against the state of Israel

Israel is a country that prides itself on being a beacon of democracy in the Middle East. With a vibrant political system, free and fair elections, and a commitment to upholding the rule of law, Israel stands as a shining example of democratic values in a region often plagued by authoritarianism and instability.

However, despite its democratic foundations, Israel is not without its challenges. One such challenge comes in the form of Arab members of parliament who espouse anti-Semitic views and work against the state of Israel. These individuals, who are elected representatives of the Arab minority in Israel, have been accused of promoting anti Semitic conspiracy theories, denying the Holocaust, and advocating for the destruction of the Jewish state.

While freedom of speech is a fundamental democratic right, the actions of these parliament members raise serious concerns about their commitment to the democratic values that Israel holds dear. By promoting anti-Semitic rhetoric and working against the interests of the state, these individuals undermine the principles of tolerance,

43

equality, and respect for diversity that are essential to a functioning democracy.

It is important to note that not all Arab members of parliament in Israel hold anti-Semitic views or work against the state. Many Arab politicians in Israel are committed to promoting the rights and interests of their constituents while also working towards a peaceful resolution to the Israeli-Palestinian conflict. These individuals play a vital role in the democratic process and contribute to the diversity and pluralism of Israeli society.

However, the actions of those Arab members of parliament who espouse anti-Semitic views and work against the state of Israel serve as a reminder of the challenges that democracy faces in a complex and divided society. It is incumbent upon all elected officials, regardless of their background or beliefs, to uphold the principles of democracy, respect the rule of law, and work towards the common good of all citizens.

In conclusion, Israel is a country that is founded on democratic values and principles. While challenges exist, such as the presence of Arab members of parliament who promote anti-Semitic views, the strength of Israel's democracy lies in its ability to confront and address these challenges through open debate, dialogue, and respect for the rule of law. By upholding these values, Israel can continue to serve as a model of democracy in the Middle East and beyond.

"In Israel there is not equal rights to different faiths"

Jews, christians, muslims , , Baha'i enjoy freedom to pray ,etc Jews, Christians, Muslims, Druze, and Bahá'í all enjoy the freedom to pray in various parts of the world. This freedom is a fundamental human right that is protected by international law and is essential for the practice of one's religion. In this essay, we will explore how these different religious groups are able to exercise their right to pray freely

44

and the importance of this freedom in promoting religious tolerance and understanding.

One of the key principles of religious freedom is the right to pray in public and private spaces without fear of persecution or discrimination. This right is enshrined in various international human rights instruments, such as the Universal Declaration of Human Rights and the International Covenant on Civil and Political Rights. These documents affirm the right of individuals to practice their religion freely and without interference from the state or other individuals.

Jews, Christians, Muslims, Druze, and Bahá'í all have different practices and rituals associated with prayer. For example, Jews pray three times a day, facing Jerusalem, while Christians may pray in churches or in private settings. Muslims pray five times a day, facing Mecca, and Druze have their own unique prayer practices. Bahá'í also have specific prayers and rituals that are central to their faith.

Despite these differences, all of these religious groups are able to practice their faith and pray freely in many parts of the world. This is due to the protection of religious freedom in many countries and the recognition of the importance of diversity and tolerance in society. In countries where religious freedom is respected, individuals are able to express their beliefs and practices without fear of reprisal or discrimination.

The freedom to pray is not only important for individuals to practice their religion, but it also plays a crucial role in promoting understanding and tolerance among different religious groups. When individuals are able to pray freely, they are more likely to engage in dialogue and exchange with others who may have different beliefs. This can help to break down barriers and stereotypes and foster a sense of unity and respect among diverse religious communities.

45

In conclusion, the freedom to pray is a fundamental human right that is essential for the practice of religion and the promotion of tolerance and understanding among different religious groups. Jews, Christians, Muslims, Druze, and Bahá'í all enjoy this freedom in many parts of the world, thanks to the protection of religious freedom in international law and the recognition of the importance of diversity and tolerance in society. It is crucial that this freedom continues to be upheld and respected in order to ensure a peaceful and harmonious coexistence among all religious communities.

"Israel committed War crimes"

The accusation that Israel has committed war crimes is a serious and damaging claim that is often made without credible evidence. This accusation is frequently promoted by individuals and organizations with a clear bias against the state of Israel, leading to the spread of misinformation and false narratives. In reality, Israel, a country that has faced constant threats to its existence since its establishment, operates with the utmost respect for international law and human rights.

The Israel Defense Forces (IDF) have consistently prioritized minimizing civilian casualties during conflicts, even at the risk of their own soldiers' lives. The IDF conducts thorough investigations and inquiries following any allegations of misconduct, demonstrating their commitment to upholding ethical standards in warfare. The sacrifices made by Israeli soldiers in their efforts to protect the Palestinian civilian population should not be overlooked, as they demonstrate a dedication to upholding moral and ethical standards in the face of adversity.

It is important to recognize that the IDF has suffered a significant number of casualties in their efforts to protect civilians, which should dispel any notion that Israel intentionally targets non-combatants or commits war crimes. The dissemination of unsupported accusations of war crimes by Israel only serves to demonize the state and perpetuate a false narrative of Israeli aggression. Those who spread these lies hinder the cause of peace and contribute to escalating tensions in an already volatile region.

In conclusion, the accusation of Israel committing war crimes lacks credible evidence and is not supported by facts. The IDF's commitment to ethical standards in warfare and protection of civilian populations is evident in their actions on the ground. It is imperative to put an end to the spread of false information and work towards a peaceful resolution to the conflict between Israel and the Palestinians. By addressing these baseless accusations and promoting a more balanced and fact-based narrative, we can move towards a more constructive dialogue and ultimately, a lasting peace in the region.

"Israel doing Ethnic cleansing "

Absurd lies and absolutely unsupported claims

47

The claim that Israel is engaging in ethnic cleansing of Palestinians is not only absurd but also completely unfounded. This accusation is often made by individuals and groups who are critical of Israel's policies and actions in the region. However, a closer examination of the facts reveals that this claim is baseless and lacks any credibility.

One of the primary reasons why the accusation of ethnic cleansing in Israel is so absurd is the fact that more than 20 percent of the population of Israel is made up of Arab citizens. These Arab citizens have the same rights and privileges as Jewish citizens and are represented in all aspects of Israeli society, including the government, the military, and the economy. This demographic reality clearly contradicts the notion that Israel is engaged in a systematic campaign to remove Palestinians from the country.

Furthermore, Israel has a long history of coexistence and cooperation with its Arab citizens. Arab citizens of Israel have the right to vote, run for political office, and participate in all aspects of Israeli society. In fact, there are Arab members of the Israeli Knesset, the country's parliament, who represent the interests of their constituents and advocate for their rights.

Additionally, Israel has made efforts to promote economic development and improve the quality of life for all of its citizens, including its Arab population. The government has invested in infrastructure projects, education, and healthcare in Arab communities, in order to ensure that all citizens have access to the same opportunities and resources.

It is important to recognize that the conflict between Israel and the Palestinians is a complex and multifaceted issue that cannot be reduced to simplistic accusations of ethnic cleansing. Both sides have legitimate grievances and concerns that need to be addressed through dialogue, negotiation, and compromise.

48

In conclusion, the claim that Israel is engaged in ethnic cleansing of Palestinians is not supported by the facts. The presence of a significant Arab population in Israel, as well as the rights and opportunities afforded to Arab citizens, clearly demonstrate that this accusation is baseless and without merit. It is essential to approach the Israeli-Palestinian conflict with a nuanced understanding of the complexities involved and to work towards a peaceful resolution that respects the rights and dignity of all parties involved.

The no democratic leaders lead the unsupported critics to Israel.

Absurd lies and absolutely unsupported claims

47

The claim that Israel is engaging in ethnic cleansing of Palestinians is not only absurd but also completely unfounded. This accusation is often made by individuals and groups who are critical of Israel's policies and actions in the region. However, a closer examination of the facts reveals that this claim is baseless and lacks any credibility.

One of the primary reasons why the accusation of ethnic cleansing in Israel is so absurd is the fact that more than 20 percent of the population of Israel is made up of Arab citizens. These Arab citizens have the same rights and privileges as Jewish citizens and are represented in all aspects of Israeli society, including the government, the military, and the economy. This demographic reality clearly contradicts the notion that Israel is engaged in a systematic campaign to remove Palestinians from the country.

Furthermore, Israel has a long history of coexistence and cooperation with its Arab citizens. Arab citizens of Israel have the right to vote, run for political office, and participate in all aspects of Israeli society. In fact, there are Arab members of the Israeli Knesset, the country's parliament, who represent the interests of their constituents and advocate for their rights.

Q

Additionally, Israel has made efforts to promote economic development and improve the quality of life for all of its citizens, including its Arab population. The government has invested in infrastructure projects, education, and healthcare in Arab communities, in order to ensure that all citizens have access to the same opportunities and resources.

48

In conclusion, the claim that Israel is engaged in ethnic cleansing of Palestinians is not supported by the facts. The presence of a significant Arab population in Israel, as well as the rights and opportunities afforded to Arab citizens, clearly demonstrate that this accusation is baseless and without merit. It is essential to approach the Israeli-Palestinian conflict with a nuanced understanding of the complexities involved and to work towards a peaceful resoluti8on that respects the rights and dignity of all parties involved.

"Israel targeting civilians Palestines intentionally

The Israel Defense Forces (IDF) have always made it a priority to minimize civilian casualties during conflicts, even at the risk of their own soldiers' lives. The IDF conducts thorough investigations and inquiries following any allegations of misconduct, demonstrating their commitment to upholding ethical standards in warfare.

It is important to recognize the sacrifices made by Israeli soldiers in their efforts to protect the Palestinian civilian population. The significant number of casualties suffered by the IDF should dispel any notion that Israel intentionally targets civilians or commits war crimes. The dedication of Israeli soldiers to upholding moral and ethical standards in the face of adversity is commendable.

The dissemination of unsupported accusations of war crimes by Israel only serves to demonize the state and perpetuate a false narrative of Israeli aggression. Those who spread these lies hinder

50

the cause of peace and only contribute to escalating tensions in an already volatile region.

In conclusion, the accusation of Israel committing war crimes lacks credible evidence and is not supported by facts. The IDF's commitment to ethical standards in warfare and protection of civilian populations is evident in their actions on the ground. It is imperative to put an end to the spread of false information and work towards a peaceful resolution to the conflict between Israel and the

51

Israel regarding its democracy values and balanced powers

Israel does not protect the minorities

The Progressive Left's misunderstanding of Israel's democracy and the systems in place to protect minorities is a concerning issue that needs to be addressed. Israel is a vibrant democracy that upholds the rights of all its citizens, regardless of their background or beliefs. The country has a robust legal system that ensures equality and protection for all individuals, including minorities

One of the key aspects of Israel's democracy is its commitment to protecting the rights of minorities. Israel is a diverse country with a significant Arab population, as well as other minority groups such as Druze, Bedouins, and Christians. These minority communities have equal rights under the law and are represented in the Israeli government and society.

Israel's legal system also provides mechanisms for addressing discrimination and ensuring that all citizens have access to justice. The Israeli Supreme Court has a strong record of upholding human rights and equality, and has ruled in favor of minority rights in numerous cases.

Furthermore, Israel has a robust system of checks and balances that ensures accountability and transparency in government. The media in Israel is free and independent, and plays a crucial role in holding the government accountable for its actions. Civil society organizations also play a vital role in advocating for the rights of minorities and promoting social justice.

52

It is important for the Progressive Left to educate themselves about Israel's democracy and the systems in place to protect minorities. By understanding the complexities of the Israeli political system and the challenges faced by minority communities, the Progressive Left can better engage with the issues facing Israel and work towards a more informed and constructive dialogue.

In conclusion, Israel is a vibrant democracy that upholds the rights of all its citizens, including minorities. The country has a strong legal system that ensures equality and protection for all individuals, and a robust system of checks and balances that promotes accountability and transparency. It is essential for the Progressive Left to educate themselves about Israel's democracy and engage in a more informed and constructive dialogue on the issues facing the country.

"BDS it's not an anti semitic instrument "

The Boycott, Divestment, and Sanctions (BDS) movement has been a topic of much debate and controversy in recent years. While proponents of BDS argue that it is a legitimate form of nonviolent resistance against Israeli policies towards Palestinians, the truth is that BDS is inherently anti-Semitic in nature. The critical thinking will argue that BDS is indeed an anti-Semitic movement, drawing parallels between BDS and historical instances of anti-Semitism.

One of the main arguments against BDS being anti-Semitic is the fact that it specifically targets Israel, the only Jewish-majority state in the world. By singling out Israel for boycotts, divestment, and sanctions, BDS effectively targets the Jewish people as a whole. This is

53

reminiscent of the Nuremberg Laws in Nazi Germany, which specifically targeted Jews for discrimination and exclusion from society. Just as the Nuremberg Laws sought to isolate and marginalize Jews, BDS seeks to isolate and delegitimize Israel on the world stage.

Furthermore, the language and tactics used by BDS supporters often echo traditional anti-Semitic tropes. For example, BDS activists frequently accuse Israel of being a "colonial" and "apartheid" state, drawing parallels between Israeli policies and those of racist regimes in history. This demonization of Israel as a uniquely evil entity is a common theme in anti-Semitic propaganda, which has historically portrayed Jews as a malevolent force in society.

Additionally, the BDS movement has been criticized for its double standards and hypocrisy when it comes to human rights abuses. While BDS supporters focus on Israel's treatment of Palestinians,

They often ignore or downplay human rights abuses committed by other countries in the region. This selective outrage against Israel, while turning a blind eye to other conflicts and atrocities, is a clear example of anti-Semitism in action.

In conclusion, the BDS movement is indeed an anti-Semitic movement that seeks to delegitimize and isolate Israel on the world stage. By singling out the Jewish state for boycotts and sanctions, using language and tactics that echo traditional anti-Semitic tropes, and displaying double standards and hypocrisy when it comes to human rights abuses, BDS reveals itself to be a modern manifestation of anti-Semitism. It is important to recognize and condemn anti Semitism in all its forms, including those disguised as political activism.

54

"If Israel move to the 1967 borders will be peace"

The ongoing conflict between Israel and its Arab neighbors has been a source of tension and violence for decades. Many have argued that if Israel were to move back to its 1967 borders, also known as the Green Line, peace would be achievable. However, the question remains: why has peace been elusive before 1967, in 1956, and even earlier in 1948 when the United Nations proposed a partition plan?

One clear answer to this question is that the Arab nations surrounding Israel have consistently rejected any attempts at peace. Instead of seeking a peaceful resolution to the conflict, they have continuously resorted to violence and aggression towards Israel. The Arab rejection of the UN partition plan in 1948 is a prime example of this. The plan aimed to divide the land into separate Jewish and Arab states, but the Arab nations rejected it, choosing instead to launch a war against Israel. This rejection of a peaceful solution set the tone for future conflicts and tensions in the region.

Similarly, in 1956, during the Suez Crisis, Arab nations once again demonstrated their unwillingness to pursue peace. Egypt, along with other Arab countries, sought to nationalize the Suez Canal, leading to a military intervention by Israel, France, and the United Kingdom. The Arab response to this crisis was one of hostility and aggression, further perpetuating the cycle of violence in the region.

Moving forward to 1967, the Six-Day War saw Israel gaining control of territories beyond the Green Line. While some argue that a return to these borders could lead to peace, the underlying issue remains the Arab rejection of Israel's right to exist. The Arab nations have consistently refused to recognize Israel as a legitimate state and have instead sought its destruction. This fundamental refusal to accept

55

Israel's existence as a sovereign nation has been a major obstacle to achieving peace in the region.

In conclusion, the lack of peace in the Middle East cannot solely be attributed to Israel's borders or actions. The root cause of the conflict lies in the Arab nations' refusal to accept Israel's right to exist and their ongoing hostility towards the Jewish state. Until the Arab nations are willing to recognize Israel's legitimacy and work towards a peaceful resolution, the cycle of violence and conflict is likely to continue. Peace will only be achievable when all parties involved are committed to dialogue, compromise, and mutual respect.

Arabs never had complicity with the Nazis and always treat jews like equals

robbery becoming more prevalent in the 18th, 19th, and 20th centuries.

One of the most significant events in the history of Jewish persecution by Arabs was the Mufti alliance with the Nazis during World War II. The Mufti of Jerusalem, Haj Amin al-Husseini, formed a close relationship with Adolf Hitler and the Nazi regime, advocating for the extermination of Jews and actively participating in the Holocaust. This alliance led to the deaths of millions of Jews and further fueled anti-Semitic sentiments in the Arab world.

In the 19th century, pogroms against Jews in the Middle East were common occurrences. These violent attacks often resulted in the destruction of Jewish communities, with many Jews being killed, raped, and robbed by Arab mobs. One notable example of this was the pogrom in Jerusalem in 1920, where Jewish residents were targeted and brutalized by Arab rioters.

In the 20th century, the violence against Jews by Arabs continued, with pogroms in Judea and Samaria becoming more frequent. These attacks were often fueled by religious and political tensions, leading to widespread destruction and loss of life within the Jewish communities. The patriarchs' tombs were also targeted during these pogroms, with many sacred sites being desecrated and destroyed by Arab extremists. Also the brutal Hebron's pogrom marks a bloody anniversary for the jewish community.

The ongoing persecution of Jews by Arabs has had a lasting impact on the Jewish community, leading to a sense of fear and insecurity.

The violence and discrimination faced by Jews throughout history have only served to strengthen their resolve and determination to persevere in the face of adversity.

58

In conclusion, the history of Jews being attacked, raped, and robbed by Arabs is a tragic and shameful chapter in human history. The alliance between the Mufti and the Nazis, the pogroms in the 19th and 20th centuries, and the ongoing violence in the Middle East serve as reminders of the deep-rooted hatred and intolerance that continues to plague our world. It is essential to remember these atrocities and work towards building a more inclusive and peaceful society for all.

"Arabs muslims have been living in peace with jews worldwide."

Throughout history, Arabs have been involved in persecuting, raping, and murdering Jews worldwide. This can be seen in the numerous pogroms that have taken place in countries such as Iraq, Yemen, Egypt, Syria, Lebanon, and Jordan. These acts of violence have been fueled by religious, political, and social tensions that have existed between Arabs and Jews for centuries.

One of the most well-known instances of Arab persecution of Jews occurred in Iraq during the Farhud pogrom of 1941. This violent event saw the massacre of hundreds of Jews in Baghdad, as well as the looting and destruction of Jewish homes and businesses. The Farhud was a result of anti-Jewish sentiment that had been brewing in Iraq for years, fueled by Nazi propaganda and the rise of Arab nationalism.

Similarly, in Yemen, Jews have faced persecution and violence at the hands of their Arab neighbors. The Jewish community in Yemen has a long history of being marginalized and discriminated against, with

59

instances of rape, murder, and forced conversion being all too common. The situation for Yemeni Jews only worsened with the rise of Islamic extremism in the region, leading to further violence and persecution.

In Egypt, Syria, Lebanon, and Jordan, Jews have also faced persecution and violence at the hands of Arabs. Pogroms, riots, and attacks on Jewish communities have been a recurring theme in these countries, with Jews being targeted for their religion, ethnicity, and perceived political allegiances. The Arab-Israeli conflict has only served to exacerbate tensions between Arabs and Jews in these countries, leading to further violence and bloodshed.

It is important to acknowledge and condemn the history of Arab persecution of Jews worldwide. These acts of violence and discrimination have had a lasting impact on Jewish communities, leading to displacement, trauma, and loss of life. By understanding the root causes of this persecution and working towards reconciliation and peace, we can strive to create a more just and inclusive society for all.

"Jews live in peace today with Muslim and arabs" jews can feel secure

The relationship between Jews and Arabs, particularly in the context of the Israeli-Palestinian conflict, has been marked by tension and conflict for decades. Jews often do not feel secure or at peace with Arab communities, both within Israel and worldwide. This lack of security and peace is exacerbated by the actions of some pro Palestinian demonstrators who target and attack Jewish synagogues, kosher shops, restaurants, and organizations.

One of the main reasons for the lack of peace and security felt by Jews in relation to Arab communities is the long-standing conflict between Israel and Palestine. The Israeli-Palestinian conflict is a complex and deeply rooted issue that has led to violence, bloodshed,

60

and animosity between the two sides. This conflict has spilled over into other parts of the world, leading to tensions between Jewish and Arab communities in various countries.

Pro-Palestinian demonstrations often serve as a platform for expressing anti-Israel sentiments, which can sometim escalate into anti-Semitic attacks on Jewish establishments. These attacks are not only physical but also psychological, as they create a sense of fear and insecurity among Jewish communities. The targeting of Jewish synagogues, kosher shops, and restaurants is a clear indication of the deep-seated animosity towards Jews that exists within some pro Palestinian groups.

Furthermore, the rise of anti-Semitism within certain Muslim communities has also contributed to the lack of peace and security felt by Jews worldwide. Anti-Semitic rhetoric and actions have become increasingly prevalent in some Muslim-majority countries, leading to a sense of vulnerability among Jewish populations. This has further strained the already fragile relationship between Jews and Arabs, making it difficult for them to coexist peacefully.

In order to address the lack of peace and security felt by Jews in relation to Arab communities, it is essential to promote dialogue, understanding, and mutual respect between the two sides. Education and awareness-raising initiatives can help combat anti-Semitism and promote tolerance and acceptance of diversity. Additionally, governments and law enforcement agencies must take swift action to address and prevent anti-Semitic attacks, ensuring the safety and security of Jewish communities.

In conclusion, the lack of peace and security felt by Jews in relation to Arab communities is a complex issue that stems from the Israeli Palestinian conflict, anti-Semitic sentiments within certain Muslim communities, and the actions of some pro-Palestinian demonstrators. It is crucial to address these underlying issues and promote dialogue

61

and understanding in order to foster peaceful coexistence between Jews and Arabs. Only through mutual respect and tolerance can we create a world where all communities can live in peace and security.

"Anti israeli movements and demonstrations are not antisemitic "

Anti-Israeli movements and demonstrations are often accused of being anti-Semitic, and in many cases, this accusation holds true. While many of them harbor anti-Semitic beliefs, it is important to remark that there is no real difference between criticism of the Israeli state and discrimination against Jewish people

One of the most prominent anti-Israel movements is the Boycott, Divestment, and Sanctions (BDS) campaign, which seeks to pressure Israel to end its "occupation of Palestinian territories." Critics of BDS argue that the movement is inherently anti-Semitic because it specifically targets Israel. However, it is crucial to recognize that criticism of Israeli policies is finally 6 to anti-Semitism. The BDS movement is inherently anti-Semitic, as its primary goal is to undermine the Jewish state

That being said, there are many instances where anti-Israel activism crosses the line into anti-Semitism. Some pro-Palestinian activists may espouse hateful rhetoric or engage in discriminatory behavior towards Jewish individuals. This type of behavior is unacceptable and should be condemned. It is essential to differentiate between legitimate criticism of Israeli policies and actions that perpetuate anti Semitic stereotypes and discrimination.

In conclusion, while it is fair to label all anti-Israel movements and demonstrations as anti-Semitic, it is important to acknowledge that there are individuals within these movements who hold anti-Semitic beliefs. It is crucial to address and confront instances of anti Semitism within these movements

"The United Nations advocacy for human rights , UNRWA and others instrument"s for helping the Palestinians refugees "

The United Nations Relief and Works Agency for Palestine Refugees in the Near East (UNRWA) has been embroiled in controversy over its alleged involvement in acts of real antisemitism, particularly in the

63

case of the October 7 massacre. This incident, which took place in 1985, saw the murder of three Israeli civilians by Palestinian terrorists in Cyprus. UNRWA has been accused of providing support to the perpetrators of this heinous act, raising serious questions about its role in perpetuating antisemitism.

The October 7 massacre was a brutal and senseless act of violence that shocked the world. Three Israeli civilians, including a mother and her two young children, were killed by Palestinian terrorists who had hijacked an Italian cruise ship. The terrorists demanded the release of Palestinian prisoners held in Israeli jails, and when their demands were not met, they carried out the cold-blooded murders.

UNRWA's involvement in this tragic event has been the subject of much scrutiny and criticism. It has been alleged that the agency provided support to the terrorists, including financial assistance and logistical help. This has raised serious concerns about UNRWA's impartiality and neutrality, as well as its commitment to upholding human rights and combating antisemitism.

Furthermore, UNRWA's involvement in the hostages taken during the October 7 massacre has also come under scrutiny. The agency has been accused of failing to protect the hostages and of not taking adequate measures to ensure their safety. This has raised questions about UNRWA's ability to fulfill its mandate of providing assistance and protection to Palestinian refugees in the region.

The allegations of UNRWA's involvement in acts of real antisemitism are deeply troubling and must be thoroughly investigated.

There are many issues that probe that horrible engagement. The agency must

be held accountable for any wrongdoing and must take immediate steps to address these serious concerns. It is imperative that UNRWA upholds the principles of impartiality, neutrality, and respect for human rights in all its operations, and that it takes concrete actions to combat antisemitism in all its forms.

64

In conclusion, the case of UNRWA's involvement in the October 7 massacre raises serious questions about the agency's commitment to combating antisemitism and upholding human rights. It is essential that UNRWA be held accountable for any wrongdoing and that it takes immediate steps to address these concerns. The agency must finish its operations and a new agency with a strong commitment to impartiality, neutrality, and respect for human rights in all its operations, and it must take concrete actions to combat antisemitism and ensure the safety and well-being of all those under its care.

"Jews stole land from arabs"

The accusation that Israeli colonists have been stealing Palestinian lands is a false and misleading claim. The truth is that there have been Jews who have been purchasing land from Arabs even before the establishment of the State of Israel. Prominent figures such as Baron Hirsh, Rothschild, and others have bought large extensions of land for agricultural purposes, and many Jewish settlers have arrived to cultivate these fields.

It is important to note that the acquisition of land by Jews in the region has been done through legal and legitimate means. The purchases were made through negotiations and agreements with the Arab landowners, and the transactions were conducted in accordance with the laws and regulations in place at the time. There was no theft or illegal seizure of land involved in these transactions.

65

Furthermore, the Jewish settlers who arrived in the region did so with the intention of building a home for themselves and establishing a community. They worked hard to cultivate the land and make it productive, contributing to the development and prosperity of the region. These settlers were not colonialists seeking to exploit or oppress the local population, but rather individuals seeking to build a better life for themselves and their families.

It is also worth mentioning that the Jewish presence in the region dates back thousands of years, long before the establishment of the State of Israel. Jews have a deep historical and cultural connection to the land, and their presence in the region is not a recent phenomenon. The Jewish people have a legitimate claim to the land based on historical, religious, and cultural ties.

In conclusion, the accusation that Israeli colonists have been stealing Palestinian lands is unfounded and misleading. The truth is that Jews have been purchasing land from Arabs through legal and legitimate means, and their presence in the region is based on historical and cultural ties to the land. It is important to understand the complexities of the situation and to avoid making simplistic and inaccurate accusations.

"Jews bring the malaria to Palestine"

Throughout history, Jews have been the target of numerous accusations and stereotypes, often based on ignorance and prejudice. One particularly rare and absurd accusation was the claim that Jews brought malaria to Palestine. This accusation is not only false but also demonstrates the lengths to which anti-Semitic rhetoric can go.

Malaria has been a significant challenge for the people of Palestine and for anyone who lived or traveled to the region. The disease is transmitted through the bite of infected mosquitoes and has been a major health concern in many parts of the world, including Palestine.

Jews, like all other inhabitants of the region, were not immune to the effects of malaria. Many fell ill, some became blind, and tragically, some even died from the disease.

To suggest that Jews were responsible for bringing malaria to Palestine is not only baseless but also illogical. Malaria is a disease that has been present in the region for centuries, long before the establishment of the State of Israel. TheAny scientific evidence does not support the accusation that Jews somehow introduced the disease to the regions is simply a manifestation of anti-Semitic sentiment.
68

Accusations like these are not only harmful but also dangerous. They perpetuate harmful stereotypes and fuel hatred and discrimination against Jewish people. It is important to challenge and debunk such baseless accusations and to educate others about the true causes of diseases like malaria.

In conclusion, the accusation that Jews brought malaria to Palestine is not only false but also a rare and absurd claim. Malaria has been a longstanding challenge for the people of the region, and Jews, like all others, have been affected by the disease. It is crucial to reject and challenge such baseless accusations and to promote understanding and tolerance among all people, regardless of their background or beliefs.

"Jews stole the Palestinians Organs"

The accusation that Jews have been stealing organs from Palestinians is not only absurd but also deeply offensive. This conspiracy theory has been circulating for years, perpetuating harmful stereotypes and fueling anti-Semitic sentiments. The idea that Jews would engage in such heinous and unethical practices is not
69
only baseless but also goes against the values and principles of Judaism.

It is important to note that there is no credible evidence to support these claims. The accusations are often based on hearsay and misinformation, and have been debunked by numerous reputable sources. In fact, the World Health Organization has stated that there is no evidence to suggest that organ trafficking is taking place in Israel or the Palestinian territories.

Furthermore, it is worth mentioning that many victims of Palestinian terror attacks have actually donated their organs to Palestinians and Israeli Arabs. Organ donation is a selfless act of kindness and generosity, and it is deeply troubling that such acts of compassion are being overshadowed by baseless accusations and conspiracy theories.

It is crucial to challenge and debunk these harmful myths and stereotypes. By spreading misinformation and promoting conspiracy theories, we are only perpetuating hatred and division. It is important to approach these issues with a critical and discerning eye, and to rely on credible sources and evidence.

In conclusion, the accusation that Jews have been stealing organs from Palestinians is not only absurd but also deeply offensive. It is crucial to challenge and debunk these harmful myths and stereotypes, and to promote understanding and compassion. Organ donation is a noble and selfless act, and it is important to recognize and celebrate the generosity of those who choose to donate their organs to save lives.

[2] terrorist groups like Hamas, which routinely target Israeli civilians with rockets and other acts of violence. Instead, the United Nations chooses to focus solely on Israeli actions, painting the country as the aggressor in the conflict.

In addition to the bias against Israel in the United Nations, other organizations like UNESCO, the Human Rights Council, and the Women's Organization have also been criticized for their unfair treatment of Israel. These organizations often single out Israel for condemnation, while turning a blind eye to the actions of other countries with far worse human rights records.

Overall, the bias against Israel in international organizations is not only unfair, but it is also counterproductive. By singling out Israel for condemnation, these organizations are not only perpetuating a one sided narrative, but they are also hindering the prospects for peace in the region. Instead of focusing solely on Israel, the United Nations and other international organizations should work towards a more

71

balanced and constructive approach to resolving the Israeli Palestinian conflict.

In conclusion, the bias against Israel in international organizations is a shameful and destructive phenomenon. The disproportionate focus on Israel, the biased resolutions, and the unfair treatment of the country all contribute to a toxic environment that hinders the prospects for peace in the region. It is time for the United Nations and other international organizations to reassess their approach to Israel and work towards a more fair and constructive dialogue.

"Arabs were first in Palestine and Jesus was Palestinian "

It is a common misconception that Arabs were the first inhabitants of Palestine and that Jesus was Palestinian. However, historical and archaeological evidence suggests otherwise. The land of Palestine has a long and complex history, with various peoples and cultures inhabiting the region over the centuries.

One of the earliest known inhabitants of Palestine were the Canaanites, who settled in the area around 3000 BC. The Canaanites were followed by the Israelites, who established the Kingdom of Israel in the region around 1000 BC. The Israelites were a Semitic people, closely related to the Arabs, but they were a distinct ethnic and cultural group with their own language, religion, and customs.

Jesus, who is a central figure in Christianity, was born and raised in the region of Judea, which is part of modern-day Israel. Jesus was a Jew, belonging to the Jewish people who had been living in the land of Israel for centuries. He practiced the Jewish faith, observed Jewish customs, and spoke the Hebrew language. There is no historical evidence to suggest that Jesus was Palestinian or that he identified as such.

The idea that Arabs were the first inhabitants of Palestine and that Jesus was Palestinian is often used to promote a particular political agenda. It is important to separate historical fact from political rhetoric and to acknowledge the complex and diverse history of the region. The land of Palestine has been home to many different peoples and cultures over the centuries, including Jews, Arabs, Christians, and Muslims.

In conclusion, it is not true that Arabs were the first in Palestine and that Jesus was Palestinian. The historical and archaeological evidence points to a much more nuanced and complex history of the region. Jesus was a Jew who lived and died in the land of Israel, and the Jewish people have a long and deep connection to the land of Palestine. It is important to understand and respect the diverse history of the region and to avoid simplifying or distorting it for political purposes.

"Arabs are the legitimate exclusive Heritage of Abraham Itzjak and Jacob "

Abraham, Itzhak, and Jacob are revered figures in both Islam and Judaism, but the claim that Islam was the first religion and that Jews took their beliefs from the Quran is simply false. Both religions have distinct histories, beliefs, and practices that have evolved over centuries.

Islam traces its origins back to the Prophet Muhammad in the 7th century CE, who received revelations from Allah that were compiled into the Quran. The religion spread rapidly throughout the Arabian Peninsula and beyond, establishing a new monotheistic faith that emphasized submission to the will of Allah. Abraham, known as Ibrahim in Islam, is considered a prophet in Islam and is revered for his unwavering faith and devotion to Allah.

Judaism, on the other hand, is one of the oldest monotheistic religions in the world, dating back to the time of Abraham, Itzhak, and Jacob in the ancient Near East. The Jewish people trace their lineage back to the patriarchs and matriarchs of the faith, who are considered the founders of the Jewish nation. The Torah, the sacred text of Judaism, contains the stories and teachings of these figures and their descendants, outlining the covenant between the Jewish people and God.

77

While there are similarities between Islam and Judaism, such as the belief in one God and the importance of ethical behavior, the two religions have distinct theological differences that have shaped their respective traditions. Islam places a strong emphasis on the teachings of the Prophet Muhammad and the Quran, while Judaism focuses on the laws and commandments found in the Torah and other sacred texts.

The claim that Jews took their beliefs from the Quran is not supported by historical evidence or religious scholarship. Judaism predates Islam by thousands of years and has its own rich tradition and heritage that have been passed down through generations. While there may be shared themes and figures between the two religions, they are distinct faiths with unique beliefs and practices.

In conclusion, Abraham, Itzhak, and Jacob are important figures in both Islam and Judaism, but the claim that Islam was the first religion and that Jews took their beliefs from the Quran is inaccurate. Both religions have deep roots in history and have developed their own distinct traditions and teachings over time. It is important to recognize and respect the unique contributions of each faith to the world's religious and cultural heritage.

Gaza the biggest jail in the world

The Palestinian claims that they have been living in a big jail in Gaza are not only absurd but also misleading. The truth is that the residents of Gaza have been living a relatively comfortable life until the outbreak of conflict in October 2007. The notion that Gaza is a prison for its inhabitants is a gross oversimplification of the complex political and social realities in the region.

It is important to acknowledge that the situation in Gaza is indeed challenging, with high levels of poverty, unemployment, and limited access to basic services. However, it is crucial to understand that these challenges are a result of the ongoing conflict between Israel and Palestine, rather than a deliberate attempt to imprison the people of Gaza.

Prior to the outbreak of conflict in 2007, Gaza was a bustling and vibrant city with a thriving economy and a rich cultural heritage. The residents of Gaza enjoyed access to education, healthcare, and other essential services, and many were able to lead fulfilling and productive lives.

The false narrative of Gaza as a prison is often perpetuated by political actors seeking to garner sympathy and support for their cause. Another significant fake news. While indeed

80

It is important to recognize that this blockade is a response to security concerns and is not intended to punish or imprison the people of Gaza.

It is also worth noting that the situation in Gaza is not solely the result of Israeli actions. The internal divisions within the Palestinian leadership, as well as the influence of extremist groups, have contributed to the instability and insecurity in the region.

In conclusion, while the challenges facing the people of Gaza are real and significant, it is important to avoid simplistic and misleading narratives that paint Gaza as a prison. The residents of Gaza are not prisoners, but rather individuals with hopes, dreams, and aspirations, who deserve to be treated with dignity and respect. It is only through a nuanced understanding of the complexities of the situation in Gaza that we can work towards a peaceful and sustainable resolution to the conflict.

Israel prevent Gaza to be the Singapure of the Middle East

Gaza, a small strip of land located on the eastern coast of the Mediterranean Sea, has often been referred to as the "Singapore of the Middle East" due to its strategic location and potential for economic development. However, the reality on the ground paints a starkly different picture, with Gaza facing numerous challenges that prevent it from achieving the level of prosperity and success seen in Singapore.

Gaza, a small strip of land located on the eastern coast of the Mediterranean Sea, has often been referred to as the "Singapore of the Middle East" due to its strategic location and potential for economic development. However, the reality on the ground paints a starkly different picture, with Gaza facing numerous challenges that prevent it from achieving the level of prosperity and success seen in Singapore.

The truth is that this dynamic of treating the Jewish state of Israel differently from other countries is, according to the IHRA definition, an act of antisemitism.

There is no proportionality regarding the israeli atack to Gaza

From a public opinion perspective, it seems that many understand that the proportional use of force is to commit the same atrocities that Hamas perpetrated against Israelis on Black Saturday in October. The Israeli army has communicated that they cannot execute such "proportionality" because they did not find any Israeli soldiers willing to violate and break the pelvis of women and girls, nor were there any Israeli soldiers willing to torture families, gouge out a father's eye, cut off a mother's breast, cut off a child's leg, and a sister's arm. There were also no Israeli soldiers willing to go house to house killing entire families, looting and plundering.

But proportionality is not an eye for an eye or a tooth for a tooth, but rather using the necessary force to achieve the objective.

The truth is that if Israel had no logistical and operational problem, they could destroy all of Gaza and kill all its inhabitants, but they risk their soldiers to have the least amount of civilian casualties.

Regarding Palestinian civilians, the responsibility lies entirely with the terrorist group Hamas. Black Saturday is the largest massacre of Jews since the closing of Auschwitz and represents a wound that may not heal for generations.

There is no army more ethical than the Israeli army; no one drops leaflets or warns by phone that they are going to bomb certain places